HOW TO THINK LIKE A MANAGER

FOR THE **CISSP** EXAM

HOW TO THINK LIKE A MANAGER

FOR THE **CISSP** EXAM

LUKE AHMED

Study Notes and Theory
A CISSP Study Guide
www.studynotesandtheory.com

Preface

"How do you think like a manager?" It is one of the most common questions asked when preparing for the CISSP exam. Using 25 CISSP practice questions with detailed explanations, this book will attempt to answer how to think like a member of a senior management team who has the goal of balancing risk, cost, and most of all, human life. The questions will take you through how to resist thinking from a technical perspective to one that is more holistic of the entire organization. Like all of Study Notes and Theory's CISSP practice questions, these questions correlate multiple high-level security concepts and require thinking like a manager. Extracting the most value comes from understanding not only which choice is correct, but more importantly, why the other choices are wrong.

The Study Notes and Theory platform is here to fine-tune and provide clairvoyance into CISSP concepts from a different perspective than traditional study material. Insight is provided into how to think like a manager, strategy and mentality during the exam, core CISSP concepts, and some essential exam knowledge. The idea is that sometimes a simple word, phrase, or statement by someone else can change our own point of view. The unique thing about the CISSP exam is that no number of books, bootcamps, practice question engines, or anything else available are even close to the questions found on the real exam. It is not about memorizing topics but understanding and being able to apply the concepts. Years of direct security experience is the recommended best resource for the CISSP exam. However, some experience can be supplemented by reading multiple information security books, watching videos, and taking thousands of practice questions.

Thank you for your time in reading this book and for your support of Study Notes and Theory.

Thank you to the following for advancing and contributing their precious time and effort to the Study Notes and Theory platform: Ahmed Khatib, Ahmed Khan, Dawood Kevar, Wala Suliman, Fadi Sodah, Prashant Mohan, Mohamed Atef, Prabh Nair, Thor Pedersen, and Zakaria Hadj.

How To Think Like A Manager for the CISSP Exam
Edited by Lori C.
© 2020 Study Notes and Theory. All Rights Reserved.
Visit the author's website at www.studynotesandtheory.com
Paperback and digital book(s) (epub and mobi) produced by Booknook.biz.

Dedicated to all the security professionals sacrificing, struggling, and staying up late nights on their journey to the CISSP.

Table of Contents

QUESTION 1

Which of the following is the most important reason to verify the media sanitization process?

A. Human error
B. Adherence to security policy
C. Confidentiality
D. Shredder calibration

Exam Strategy and Mentality

Get your exam mentality in gear to face four choices that seemingly are correct, but only one will be the ultimate high-level answer. Focus on the words "most important reason".

The new CISSP computer adaptive testing (CAT) style exam was implemented on December 18, 2017[1]. Now you have a maximum of three hours to complete the exam instead of the previous six hours. Whether you have just started studying for the exam, or are a few days away from it, take your time with practice questions. You will not be able to go back and review questions on the real exam anymore.

With this and all other questions, argue with yourself over why choice A, B, C, or D is the most important reason. Alternatively, you can also take this practice question and look for the least important reason first. This technique increases your chances of getting the question correct by eliminating a choice that may seem less important than the others, while getting you closer to the most important reason. If shredder calibration is less important than accounting for human error, choice D can be eliminated.

At a high-level, the least important reason would have a lower impact on the three core foundations of security: confidentiality, integrity or availability. The most important reason would have a wider impact.

Think Like a Manager

A manager would go with the choice which, if not considered, would have the most negative impact to not only the media sanitization process, but also every other type of process.

Types of Media Sanitization

Clearing - To overwrite and replace confidential data spaces on media with something meaningless using approved software or hardware technology[2].

Purging - To completely overwrite data on a disk by degaussing or firmware commands which would lead data to be unrecoverable with a high level of confidence[3].

Destruction - Physical destruction is the only way to truly make data unrecoverable and to render the media useless. Destruction methods include shredding, pulverizing, disintegration, and incineration[4].

Exam Essentials

Look for the choice that plays an all-encompassing and authoritative role in all of the other remaining choices.

Sometimes it helps to change the question to what it really wants us to know:

"Why does the CISSP exam want me to know the most important reason to verify that there is no data leftover after sanitization?"

A. There will always be mistakes
B. Nothing happens without a policy
C. Secrets must be kept confidential
D. Proper operation of shredding devices

Study Notes and Theory's CISSP practice questions are complex for a reason: to prepare you for the real exam. It works in your favor to really break down the question and the given choices. It's important to get the question correct, but it's more important to understand why the other choices are wrong. The real exam does not care whether you can memorize encryption ciphers, OSI model protocol numbers, or the steps of the software development life cycle. The exam tests whether you can apply those concepts.

A. Human error

Humans will always make mistakes. This is not the most important reason, but it is one reason we should verify that data has been totally sanitized without a shred of data remanence. Data custodians can make mistakes when sanitizing data or any other process that requires human involvement. In addition to the verification process post-sanitization, proper personnel training should be conducted pre-sanitization to ensure adequate skill and competency[5].

B. Adherence to security policy

A security policy produced by the leadership team contains the direction, scope, and general structure in which an organization will maintain, secure, and define the acceptable risk thresholds of their information system. Policies address potential threats, along with the strategies to mitigate and recover from them. It could disrupt internal stability if the policies and directives of the company leadership are ignored. This in turn could lead to the inability to deal with external instability. Policies must be followed, as they are what allows an organization to actually *remain* organized while moving forward with revenue-driven momentum[6].

A policy document will not go into specifics (that responsibility falls on supporting documents such as standards, baselines, guidelines, procedures)[7], but will serve as the high-level directive on whether data should be cleared, purged, destroyed, or any other method the business requires. It will be the basis on whether systems should be rendered useless after use or if they should be sanitized for reuse. Adhering to the security policy is the most important reason to verify the sanitization process as it will answer the who, what, when, and why. B is the only choice that ideally would include accounting for human error, upholding confidentiality, and the maintenance of physical destruction devices in a policy and any other supporting document such as a standard, baseline, or procedure.

Security policies are mandatory if an organization wants to provide direction and show support of their protection of security issues[8].

C. Confidentiality

Confidentiality is one of the core foundations upon which security is built, along with integrity and availability. Hard drives that contain residual data even after sanitization methods have been performed would breach confidentiality, making choice C the next best choice. Why is choice B more important than choice C? Because it takes a data security policy from senior management to initiate a data classification process - to label something as "confidential". A policy is what essentially determines which data is to be classified as confidential, sensitive, private, or any other classification[9].

Core CISSP Concept

Nothing happens without a policy from within an organization on the CISSP exam, or real life. From a security governance perspective, a policy shows support from senior management. Financially, it shows the organization is willing to allocate the necessary funds to support the policy.

D. Shredder calibration

A hard drive shredder does one thing: it shreds. It does not shred some or a portion of the data, it shreds everything. There is less worry about the result of a hard drive shredder containing data remanence than the other three choices. The sanitization method of physical destruction provides visual and absolute verification, there is nothing to check afterwards except pieces of metal. For added security, material unrelated to the original data can be mixed in to add another level of confusion in case of reconstruction efforts[10]. Choice D is the least important reason to verify the sanitization process.

Think Like a Manager

Data is not recoverable after going through a shredder, and neither is a hard drive. Physical destruction is not an option if the organization wants to save money and reuse media. Always think about saving money while also trying to maximize security. If the business does not make money, there will be no security.

Rymar Tech's management would like to prepare a baseline of risks to their organization. They will need to identify the vulnerabilities that can be exploited from the events originating from various threat sources. This information will be further analyzed to determine the likelihood of occurrence and the impact it will have on the company's operations, assets, and information security in general.

A formal executive briefing will be held to report and share the results of the assessment with mission owners and information system managers. If ongoing assessments become required to monitor changes to the established baseline, the initial report will be properly maintained to reflect changes in risk factors affecting the organization.

What is the primary reason for management's new initiative?

A. Providing risk oversight

B. Making risk-based decisions

C. Selecting controls

D. Performing due diligence

Exam Strategy and Mentality

Understanding the definition of the word "primary" will provide the necessary clairvoyance for choosing the correct answer to this and any other CISSP practice question:

primary **adjective**₁

1 *Of chief importance*

2 *Earlier in time or order*

Policies or initiatives are not created for the sake of security, a primary business justification always comes first. The correct choice will serve as the overall reason for the new initiative, whereas the other choices can be ordered chronologically to support the primary reason. Initiatives are created to ultimately maintain the momentum and progress of the organization₂.

A specific and important process is occurring at Rymar Tech that has many revisions, methods, and steps outlined in CISSP study guides as well as NIST documents. But in essence, it is the same general process. Looking at each line of the question, the following words hint to the process: "prepare", "identify", "likelihood", "impact", "report", "monitor", and "maintained".

Hint: This particular process can be adjusted to suit each organization, but the primary concept is the same. What process is occurring in the question? Is it a(n):

- Evaluation
- Analysis
- Assessment
- Mitigation
- Monitoring
- Documenting

Exam Essentials

If you are still unsure of the answer, take this time to research each choice individually. The habit of researching each choice goes a long way in preparing for the real exam. It is like performing your own due care and due diligence. Taking practice questions is due care for the exam, and studying topics that still are unclear is performing due diligence.

The word "baseline" identifies a purpose, not a primary reason. Risk assessments can establish a baseline, perform an ongoing reassessment, or re-evaluate controls as a response to new risks. Whether a baseline is established to define a required level of security or an enhancement of the current one₃, the correct choice will remain the same.

A. Providing risk oversight

Risk oversight is a proactive process that starts with the board of directors. The board has the ultimate task of overseeing the risk management operations and processes that will be managed by the senior executives[4]. The new initiative is at the directive of Rymar Tech's management who are going to make risk-based decisions from the results of a risk assessment. The board will hold management accountable for a proper enterprise risk management system to determine the organization's risk appetite.

B. Making risk-based decisions

The process performed in the question is a baseline risk assessment. The assessment results will provide a benchmark of current security controls, which will be used to make risk-based decisions for the enterprise[5]. Risk oversight stakeholders use assessments to perceive uncertainties and manage risk before they become an operational surprise that affects the business function. The primary reason for Rymar Tech's new initiative is to make risk-based decisions through a baseline risk assessment. Further scoping and tailoring of baseline controls can be conducted to supplement future risk management activities.

Following are the steps of a risk assessment[6]:
- Prepare for the assessment
  - Identify purpose, scope, sources, constraints, risk model
  - A reason is needed to put energy toward the assessment
- Conduct the assessment
  - Identify threats, vulnerabilities, likelihood, impact
  - Gather information on risks and their priority level
- Communicate risk assessment information
  - Share assessment results for overall risk decision making
  - The content of the report or briefing will guide risk decisions
- Maintain the risk assessment
  - Preservation and maintenance allow document availability
  - Baseline assessment serves as a comparison to future change

Some of the risk-based decisions as a result of a risk assessment exercise can include[7]:
- Modification of existing controls
- Implementation of security solutions for the supply chain
- The discontinuation or suspension of a business function
- Changes since the last risk assessment

Core CISSP Concept

The value of a risk assessment diminishes over time. As organizations introduce more assets, operations, functions, and processes, more risk will be introduced. This is what is meant by never being able to fully eliminate risk. It's only a matter of time until one risk is replaced by another.

C. Selecting controls

A baseline risk assessment identifies the controls currently in place. Changes to an organization require another risk assessment, after which new controls will be selected to either adjust the existing baseline controls or implement new ones. This is not the correct answer because the primary initiative is to first have a baseline risk assessment to account for existing controls, whereas the need for selecting additional controls comes afterwards[8].

D. Performing due diligence

Going through an in-depth focused risk assessment, allocating time, expending effort, and practicing a posture of doing everything possible to prepare for unforeseeable risk is performing due diligence. Due diligence is not an initiative, it's an attitude. It comes with being proactive about researching long-term plausible threats.

Think Like a Manager

Risk-based decisions can cover multiple echelons of the risk management hierarchy. These include the organization itself, internal processes, and the overall information security management system. An evolving business requires ongoing cycles of risk assessment.

Gerard and Troy work at DS Technology, an industrial startup company specializing in building a Dyson Sphere. Currently, they have a satellite in the deepest reaches of space analyzing and sending back an immense amount of cosmic data. When the telemetry data comes in, Gerard has to classify it as important, useful, or negligible. To make things a bit easier on Gerard, Troy has volunteered to help his co-worker transfer, archive, mark, label, and backup all pertinent data to an external location.

As they gain more funding to continue their work, DS Technology has been asked to implement proper security governance, structure, and roles. To make sure all the spatial data is organized, valued, and available at all times, a new data classification policy also needs to be created.

What would be Gerard's role after the policy has been issued?

A. Data User

B. Data Owner

C. Data Custodian

D. Data Processor

Exam Strategy and Mentality

Out of the four choices, which are the terms you are most familiar with from your CISSP study guides? More than likely, it is the terms "data owner" and "data custodian". Focus on these two terms and look back at Gerard and Troy's roles at DS Technology before they had to implement a data classification policy. Does it make a difference that Gerard is classifying data while Troy is archiving and backing up the data? Also note that "more funding" means the company is doing well and their data is becoming more valuable. With value, comes the need for data privacy and the roles that are responsible for its protection. Think of which role has the ultimate responsibility of protecting privacy after the new data classification policy.

 ### Exam Essentials

Master the critical skill of eliminating two choices to increase your chances of getting the question correct.

Answer the question in your mind first and then look to see if it matches any of the given choices. It's tiring, but taking CISSP practice questions shouldn't feel like a chore that you just want to finish and move on. Treat each practice question as if it is the real exam. Any sentence, phrase, term, or concept you do not recognize, proceed to study and nail those unknowns until you are confident in the subject matter. Take the time now to fully research and learn any unfamiliar topics to be better prepared for the real exam later on, it's worth it.

 ### Think Like A Manager

Does Gerard's current responsibilities seem closest or furthest away from senior management? Answer this first to determine his new role. Hint: Gerard will become Troy's boss when a proper security governance structure is administered. Gerard will be in management whereas Troy will be in operations. Three out of the four choices are closely tied together whereas one is the outlier. Which three terms are used internally to an organization and which leftover term is commonly associated with an external entity? Also understand that a data owner is not the same thing as data ownership[1].

A. Data User

A data user is just someone who uses the data within an organization for their job function[2]. It takes the data owner, custodian, systems administrator, information security officer, and senior management to make sure information for the data user is[3]:

- Accurate, relevant, and updated
- Within scope of the data user's business purpose
- Contains appropriate security controls, e.g., passwords, access control lists, rights, permissions, classification, access
- Compliant and within regulatory bounds

B. Data Owner

One of the primary responsibilities of the data owner is to classify a specific set of data[4]. Classifying the data means to decide which information is or is not valuable. Gerard was the first to "classify" the data when there was no formal data classification policy at DS Technology. He is doing so using an informal classification scheme of "important, useful, or negligible." When Gerard takes on a more formal role as the data owner, he will use the more traditional classification labels associated with organizations.

Core CISSP Concept

A key difference to know for classification labels is that a private business will most commonly use the labels of "confidential", "private", "sensitive", or "public". Government agencies or the military will use the terms "top secret", "secret", "sensitive but unclassified", or "unclassified"[5].

Assigning classifications and labels is the job of a data owner. The words "organized" and "valued" hinted to the fact a data owner is required. Classification organizes data into different subsets that are dependent on their value. The higher the value, the higher the classification. The words "available at all times" hints to the primary responsibility of a data custodian: upholding availability. This is done through marking, labeling, or backing up data.

A data owner organizes and assigns values to data, and a data custodian sets up security controls to ensure data remains available to each business function. As DS Technology grows into a bigger company, and given their current responsibilities, Gerard would be the data owner and Troy would be the data custodian. In exam language, the data owner is ultimately responsible for the data and for classifying the data. While initially Troy volunteered to help Gerard, the data owner also would assign the responsibilities of the data custodian. With proper governance, Gerard would assign Troy to be a data custodian[6].

C. Data Custodian

Troy is the data custodian because he initially helped to archive the data (think availability and a proper archiving process). More importantly, he put the useful data to an external server which provides a method to ensure there is no single point of failure in case of a disaster - this upholds availability[7]. Troy deals with maintaining the data for availability, and not classifying the data. Troy's responsibility is closest to the role of someone in security operations and furthest away from senior management[8].

D. Data Processor

In terms of the General Data Protection Regulation (GDPR), if a company collects personal information, they are a data controller[9]. Think of a data processor as a third-party legal entity or agency that handles the data given to them by a data controller. These terms are synonymous with the topic of personal data privacy within the GDPR. The GDPR states third-party data processors must ensure the privacy of the data they are handling and implement security controls such as encryption, tokenization or pseudonymization[10]. Both Gerard and Troy work within DS Technology and are handling their own data, nobody is processing it for them. Additionally, DS Technology is not handling private user data, only data from space. Data processor is a term external to an organization while the other choices are internal.

Theorized by Freeman Dyson, a Dyson Sphere is a mega structure built around a star to harness its energy for near-infinite power[11].

A security consultant has been urgently hired by a bank to discover any unknown and exploitable weaknesses within their business. As it was a long holiday weekend, half the workforce as well as senior management were not available. The consultant decided to take proactive measures and begin her activities.

The consultant first gathered preliminary intelligence on the target through various automated scanning tools. She then gained access to one of the internal networks by tunneling traffic through a remote VPN (virtual private network) connection. After exploiting several other vulnerabilities within the organization's servers and databases, the consultant managed to freely traverse multiple areas of the environment gathering the maximum amount of data possible. Once enough information was collected, she removed all traces of her presence in the breached networks. On the following business day, she encrypted the results of her security test and sent the password-protected report to the bank's senior management team.

Which of the following was conducted by the security consultant?

A. Vulnerability scanning   C. Hacking

B. Penetration testing   D. Ethical hacking

Exam Strategy and Mentality

Choices A, B, and D sound similar, right? All three of these choices appear to be something a security consultant would be hired to do for an organization. But because they are three different choices, they must have properties that set them apart.

For choice C, the security consultant does not seem like she is hacking the organization, or is she? If the answer is choice C, is there anything in the context of the question to make it sound like she has ulterior motives? Or could she just be a victim of circumstance?

It seems like she is going through the steps of someone with the role of a penetration tester or ethical hacker[1]:

- Gathering intelligence via scanning tools
- Identifying and exploiting vulnerabilities
- Gaining access to the network
- Erasing evidence of intrusion
- Sending report to senior management

These also seem like the systematic and chronological steps a security professional or a hacker would take to compromise security controls. Yet, a major task draws the line between a hacker and an ethical hacker.

Hint: Has the first and last step of the penetration testing process been followed by the consultant? Aside from finding and exploiting weaknesses, these two steps serve to formally validate the overall process. Which choice would provide a true test of a company's protection mechanisms?

Think Like A Manager

What process was broken by the consultant that may or may not discredit all her work? What crucial step did the security consultant forget to do that can lead to a legal issue?

A. Vulnerability scanning

Vulnerability scanning is a part of the overall vulnerability assessment process. It can be technical in nature using various tools to look for weaknesses in devices such as routers, firewalls, or servers. Using scanners is an easier and faster method than using manual methods with human involvement[2]. They can also in turn provide a list of targets for further penetration testing. Scanners have some limitations in that they use a database of signatures to match for existing vulnerabilities[3]. These signatures need to be updated on a consistent basis and especially right before a scan. An organization should maintain a regular signature, version, or firmware upgrade schedule in order to avoid surprises.

Choice A would be correct in the sense that vulnerability scanning was conducted by the consultant. She performed vulnerability scanning by using "various automated scanning tools". But the choice actually is incorrect because without obtaining permission first, in the eyes of the law, those automated tools were just used for hacking.

B. Penetration testing

Penetration testing goes beyond a vulnerability scan. One of the key differences between choice A and choice B is that vulnerabilities can actively be exploited in a penetration test, whereas vulnerabilities are just meant to be discovered in a vulnerability scan. Penetration testing takes a high degree of skill and can cause real-world damage to real-world systems. Given this, they also are one of the best ways to determine an organization's ability to react to real-world threats[4]. Following are the general steps of a penetration test[5]:

Plan the process - Establish goals, scope, and rules. Make sure to first get management approval in writing.

Gather target intelligence - Identify IP addresses, port numbers, network drives, host names, applications, or employee information.

Exploit vulnerabilities - Successful exploitation is the core of a penetration test.

Provide report - Documentation is maintained throughout all the previous steps. A final report is then securely sent to stakeholders with accompanying mitigation techniques.

The final report will serve to determine the ability for the organization to tolerate real-world attacks, gauge the level of skill required, understand defensive capabilities, and add any additional security controls that can be used to thwart future attacks[6]. The security consultant followed the proper steps, except for the most important first step: obtaining written permission from the bank's senior management team to touch their systems.

C. Hacking

The correct answer is C, the security consultant was hacking the bank. If the bank hired the security consultant to exploit their weaknesses, how come she still is considered to be hacking? In order to "hack" an organization within legal bounds, one must first get permission from senior management. In this case, even though the security consultant was being proactive about her urgent job, she did not wait for formal written permission from the senior management of the bank who were on holiday.

Core CISSP Concept

There's only one difference between hacking and penetration testing: **permission**. A core CISSP concept is that you must **always get written permission and scope** before conducting any kind of testing that involves exploiting an organization's production environment[7]. As far as the police or FBI are concerned, this is hacking. The consultant could go to prison under the Computer Fraud and Abuse Act if within the United States (not just jail, but **prison**).

D. Ethical hacking

The terms ethical hacking and penetration testing can be related, but are not mutually exclusive. They are both an attempt to actively exploit the weaknesses within an organization's system[8]. Just because someone is an ethical hacker doesn't also mean they are a penetration tester, and vice versa. An ethical hacker is one who understands the path a real hacker may take to attack a system, but does not do so illegally or for personal gain - they follow a code.

You are presented with a pop-up screen after logging into a Windows 10 operating system at your new job as a network security engineer. It states the following:

Welcome to Rymar Tech! To remotely manage our firewalls, you will need to first generate a public and private key. In order to do so, please follow these steps:

1. Open PuTTYgen[1] from your desktop
2. Click "Generate"
3. Wave around your mouse in the box for increased complexity
4. Put in a passphrase to protect your private key (!!DO NOT <u>EVER</u> SHARE THIS PASSPHRASE!!)
5. Save public key and send it to the security department: security[at]rymartech.com
6. Save private key to your machine

This is an example of what type of company document?

A. Policy
B. Standard
C. Guideline
D. Procedure

Exam Strategy and Mentality

This is a straightforward question with straightforward choices. A policy is a high-level document with high-level language. Standards and guidelines go into more detail, and procedures are an official order of steps[2].

The pop-up screen is most likely configured by a systems administrator who would work in the IT operations department. All the given documents in the choices may be occasionally viewed by those who work in a technical capacity, however, which document would they actually use as a way to accomplish a task?

Think Like A Manager

Is the pop-up screen you encounter after logging into your computer something you need to do or have the option to do? Does it need to be done in order to do your job?

Know the differences in the four documents as they lay the written instructions for how the company operates. The documents go from high-level administrative directives to low-level technical instructions. They work together in a top-down style starting from policy, standard, baseline, guideline, and procedure[3].

Core CISSP Concept

Users are not always provided with all company documents. To be useful and effective, documents must be readily available to all users.

All types of internal public documents must be proactively updated and available to be viewed. If a user needs SSH keys to do their job, the company must provide documentation for them to do so.

Hint: One of the choices is a document that does not have to be followed, it is a strongly advised suggestion.

A. Policy

Policies are high-level documents written by senior management. They can begin with a general announcement by the leadership of the organization on the importance and commitment to security. A security policy does not go into specifics by naming individuals or their specific roles, but more about their responsibilities, why it's required, and what will happen if it is not followed[4]. You will not see the steps to create a public/private key pair written in a policy. Policies are the master security framework upon which standards, baselines, procedures, and guidelines are based[5]. Policies are official, there is no choice but to follow them. The other documents are to be crafted to only support and follow the policy. There can be three types of policies: regulatory, advisory, or informative[6].

Company documents usage examples:
- **Policy**
- Example: *Information traveling over Rymar Tech's computer network should be available to support business functions.*
    - **Standard**
    - Example: *Firewalls must be clustered with high-availability capabilities in an active/ standby pair.*
        - **Procedure**
        - Example: *Open PuTTY sessions to both firewalls*
        Configure VRRP on primary firewall
        Configure VRRP on secondary firewall
        Set priority on primary firewall to 100
        Set priority on secondary firewall to 90
        Save configuration on primary
        Save configuration on secondary
        Log out of PuTTY sessions to both firewalls
            - **Guideline**
            - Example: *If failover does not occur, manually increase priority on the secondary firewall to initiate a failover.*
                - **Baseline**
                - Example: *Firewalls should be hardened per NIST per 800-41[7], specifics before being put into production.*

B. Standard

Standards present a uniformed and efficiently managed enterprise that benefits from better consistency, integration, and a higher quality of data and systems management[8]. In other words, it is easier for a company to maintain users who are all on the same operating system (Windows) instead of having a heterogeneous environment (Linux, macOS, Ubuntu). It saves time, money, and is logistically easier to apply updates, buy software, or plan for end-of-life devices.

Think Like A Manager
An organization can deviate from a standard and have exceptions. If this occurs, then compensating controls need to be in place to mitigate the risk from the absence of the baseline control. Deviations from set company standards takes bold leadership, comprehensive due diligence, and a mixture of ideas.

C. Guideline

The definition of guidelines is easy to remember because it's the only statement that is recommended[9] - guidelines are not enforced. Consider guidelines as a helpful suggestion. You can either follow guidelines or not, but remember they are based on some of the best practices and methods in the security industry.

D. Procedure

Procedures contrast with other high-level documents by providing specific and detailed step-by-step instructions[10] to accomplish a task, such as setting up a public/private key pair using PuTTYgen. Procedures are enforced and must be followed. Procedures are repeatable, detailed, and created for all users, not just for IT security.

Core CISSP Concept
If you need to know why you have to do something within a company, look at policies. If you need to know what configurations are mandatory, check standards. If you need to know how to do something, check procedures. For all other helpful suggestions and best practices, check guidelines.

A software startup company has experienced massive growth over the last three years. Senior management and the recruiting department have been scrambling to hire more in-house developers, but customer demands still are not being met. The organization has decided to outsource the work to a third-party software development vendor. Before that, they have to perform their due diligence.

Which of the following should take place first with the third-party company?

A. Confirm compliance, privacy policy, governance, and SDLC
B. Verify the CMMI level
C. Calculate deadlines and assurances of completion
D. A risk assessment for the outsourced process

Exam Strategy and Mentality

Choices A, B, C, and D are all important things to do before outsourcing business processes to any type of third-party company. It's tough to eliminate two choices in this question as all of them appear to be correct. You have to pick the one that must occur "first". In cases like this, look for the choice that operates to encompass all the other choices.

Choice A

Compliance and privacy probably are the most important as they deal with abiding by the law of the land. The second canon of the (ISC)² Code of Ethics states, *"Act honorably, honestly, justly, responsibly, and legally"*[1]. A security professional must act legally and within the bounds of the land upon which they are rendering services. The law always will supersede any of an organization's internal policies. These two terms also are important because violations of compliance and privacy can result in a monetary fine.

Hint: If security considerations are not made at the beginning of a venture, those risks can remain throughout the span of the project.

The importance of governance goes beyond a formal establishment of senior executive leadership. Security governance is a statement that says a company not only is serious about data protection, a risk management program, or keeping security throughout their business functions, but also that it is being monitored and verified[2].

Choice B

The Capability Maturity Model Integration (CMMI) provides a framework for vendors to continuously increase the maturity of their software development methods, procedures, processes, and overall principles. It is not enough to want to have bet-

ter security, but to know how to plan for it[3]. An organization that tries to be better than it was the day before is one that takes their security development seriously. But should the verification of a CMMI take place *first?*

Choice C

There is an urgency for the startup company to find a vendor who can quickly start to meet customer deadlines. Choice C is exactly what the startup is looking for a software vendor to do for them. But is this consideration the first thing that should take place? In terms of the exam and information security in general, should this chronologically occur before any of the other choices? Should the startup be talking business before doing their due diligence?

Choice D

Understanding the risks before going into any venture is a prime example of a company performing proper due diligence. It is especially important when it comes to third-party organizations who are outside the bounds of your own organization's policies and best practices. A business exposes themselves to financial, reputational, operational, legal, and regulatory risk when engaging with a third-party[4]. Would this be a good reason for a risk assessment *first?*

A. Confirm compliance, privacy policy, governance, and SDLC

It's a must to confirm third-party vendor frameworks for compliance, privacy guidelines, governance structure, and their software development life cycle. It is the confirmation of these factors that enables a customer to verify whether the company they are doing business with is reputable with a strong security foundation. It also can expose whether the vendor shows a professional front-end to customers, but in reality, has chaotic and unmanaged backend business structures without a proper maturity level[5].

B. Verify the CMMI level

The CMMI defines the evolutionary steps of an organization from the Initial phase (Maturity Level 1) of process improvement, all the way to the Optimized phase (Maturity Level 5)[6]. A company's CMMI level helps it stand out as either a company that adheres to a proven process, or one that does not.

C. Calculate deadlines and assurances of completion

Requirements, deadlines, and assurances of completed work can be defined in the service level agreement (SLA). An SLA presents a contractual obligation of work between a customer and a vendor[7]. It is a way of making sure the customer and the vendor both know where one's responsibility ends and where the other one begins.

D. A risk assessment for the outsourced process

Risks to an organization go beyond their own domain and spills into the ecosystem of their third-party relationships where there is little to no visibility. Third-party risk assessments proactively measure[8]:

- The impact a vendor's failure has on a company's own business
- The quality, timeliness, and effect of missed deadlines
- Vendor's susceptibility to bribery, corruption, or data breach

Whether it's the completion of a vendor self-evaluation or an active on-site inspection, it is important to perform a full third-party risk assessment before any kind of contractual agreement. Risk assessments are a way to measure the level of assurance provided by the third-party for their product or service[9].

Core CISSP Concept

Calculating the amount of risk an organization is willing to tolerate should be considered before any kind of partnership, venture, purchase, acquisition, development, or initiative. Before deciding to do anything in security, perform due diligence and calculate the risks involved.

Choice A may be performed as a part of choice D. A risk assessment may already conduct a thorough check of third-party documentation based on their regulatory compliance, privacy policies, corporate governance, and software development life cycle processes. This type of assessment would provide better visibility and a more realistic view of the vendor. Third-party assessments also provide high-level oversight so the startup can make business decisions that help to continue its growth without experiencing deceleration from issues that are not even related to their own organization[10].

Choice B may occur as a part of a risk assessment checklist.

For choice C, calculating deadlines and assurances of completion are parameters that would be more included in an SLA. At its core, an SLA should address security, quality of work, timely completion, and penalties if services are not met[11]. This is not the first step and occurs after the completion of a risk assessment when the startup agrees to and feels comfortable with the third-party and their business operations.

Think Like A Manager

Choice D is thinking like a manager. The CISSP exam wants a manager to think at a high level to make sure the proper processes are in place before any action or procurements are started. As it affects the entire organization, ensuring a risk assessment is performed should be the first step in the outsourcing process. Business is business, so when it comes to information security, your partners' problems also are your problems. Ideally, trust but verify.

Rymar Tech is in a position to acquire a sports agency for $8.24 billion. The CFO will create the financial statements of the agency's tangible and intangible assets, goodwill, liabilities, and total purchase price. The documents will be sent to the legal and accounting team of both companies who will perform their due diligence. After agreement, the documents will be formally approved by the CEOs of both entities. The security requirements are that all financial statements, records, and contracts are protected from alteration. Neither party is to directly modify, send, or receive any documents on their own. A custom system application is currently being created to facilitate this process and meet the security objectives.

Which security model should be used for the system?

A. Clark-Wilson (CW)

B. Bell-LaPadula (BLP)

C. Brewer and Nash (B&N)

D. Biba

Exam Strategy and Mentality

The security professional and future CISSP should have a deep understanding of how these models are engineered. If you did not know the term "security model", then the choices have shown you. Sometimes an exam not only tests us, but also teaches us a great deal. Perhaps you studied all the choices but did not know they were referred to as security models. Or maybe you studied BLP and Biba but just couldn't fully understand CW and B&N. At their core, these models teach two basic fundamentals of security enforcement: prevent data disclosure (confidentiality)[1], deny unauthorized subjects from changing objects, keep the accuracy of data, and maintain the consistency of the data on our computers with that of our own reality (integrity)[2].

Each of the security models holds their own special property: confidentiality, integrity, separation of duties, or resolving conflict of interest[3]. What would be the most important property for this financial acquisition? Do the security policy requirements state it is important to make sure nobody sees the purchase price and other financial numbers? Is it important to make sure financial statements on a balance sheet are accurate? Is it important that both parties do not get too much power in what duties they can perform? Would a conflict of interest totally cause the acquisition to flop?

Whichever the case, please note whereas the core principles do not change, security models are not rigid in their approach. Each can be adopted differently depending on the company security policy.

Hint: Look at the word "alteration" and "directly modify". The security model that provides a combination of both these terms will be the correct answer.

Is one choice clearly the incorrect answer? Do two choices work to uphold the same principle, but only one goes further to enforce an additional principle? Can you determine whether one of the choices could work in this type of financial acquisition, but does not quite meet the interpretation of the security requirements? You may never encounter these models in your career, or may be using them without knowing it. Either way, understanding their primary purpose will provide more insight into the security field in general and the exam. Which choice would work the best to make sure financial numbers are kept consistent?

A. Clark-Wilson

The Clark-Wilson model has some complex terminology, but it is a special security model to understand. Following are the components:

User: Subjects who want to access an object.

Transformation Procedure (TP) - Used to perform limited read, write, and change operations as a well-formed transaction on a CDI.

Constrained Data Item (CDI) - Data object that can only be modified by a TP, never the user. CDIs are objects of high importance and require the maintenance of their integrity at all times.

Unconstrained Data Item (UDI) - Data object with less importance than a CDI and can be directly modified by a user.

Integrity Verification Procedure (IVP) - Confirms the integrity and consistency of the CDI after modification. Audits and logs the TP_4.

When it comes to CW, think of the access triple. An authenticated subject (user) can only access or change an important object (CDI) by going through a middle interface (TP)-this enforces separation of duties. An IVP then audits the work of the TP and checks the consistency of the internal change on the CDI with what is expected externally. Clark-Wilson works to uphold the three requirements for integrity, which is integrity itself, access control, and auditing[5].

This model should be used for the new system because the CFO (user) will create and send (TP) financial statements (CDI) to different entities. The CEOs (users) will then approve (TP) the documents (CDI). If there were documents considered UDIs, the CEOs and CFO would be able to modify them directly without going through a TP. Whether large-scale corporate acquisitions or a simple billing invoice, inconsistent numbers will ruin the entire transaction.

Core CISSP Concept

A security policy uses conceptual language to state business requirements. A security model takes these requirements and uses mathematics and programming to match the policy to the system. Executives demand it, programmers provide it[6].

B. Bell-LaPadula

This choice could have been eliminated right away as the Bell-LaPadula model is only meant to uphold confidentiality. It is primarily used in military or government sectors where maintaining a secret can be of national importance. For BLP, preventing the disclosure of information is more important than the alteration of it. Here is how it is done:

Simple Security Rule - A lower level subject cannot read confidential objects from a higher level, they cannot read up.

Star Property Rule - A higher level subject cannot write to data at a lower level, they cannot write down.

Strong Star Property - A subject can only read and write to data objects in their own security level, not higher or lower[7].

C. Brewer and Nash

Dynamic by nature and meant to prevent the disclosure of confidential data, B&N is mainly intended to avoid conflicts of interest. If the security requirements stated to prevent subjects who currently have or will inherit access to secret information with both Rymar Tech[8] and the sports agency, the correct answer would be C. The requirements were to uphold integrity and separation of duties.

D. Biba

While the Biba model does address integrity, it does not practice separation of duties. Even so, integrity is maintained for subject-to-object access with data flowing directly between higher and lower integrity level subjects. Rymar Tech could have used the Biba model, but the requirements were that nobody except a middle interface was to conduct actions. Following are the Biba Model's properties:

Star Integrity Axiom - Subjects cannot write data up to a higher level, they cannot write up.

Simple Integrity Axiom - Subjects cannot read data from a lower level, they cannot read down.

Invocation Property - Subjects cannot invoke the services of objects in a higher integrity. Think of it as a simple way to keep data clean[9].

QUESTION 8

A company has made significant configuration changes that would protect them from most Open Systems Interconnection (OSI) Layer 4 attacks. From which attacks are they still vulnerable?

I. SYN flood
II. Smurf Attack
III. Fraggle Attack
IV. Ping flood

A. III, IV
B. I, II
C. II, III
D. II, IV

Exam Strategy and Mentality

This may seem like a short and simple question, but it tests your knowledge of the OSI model. Not only do you have to know each layer and function, but also at which OSI layer each type of attack would occur.

Exam Essentials

Each communication device, protocol, technology, or network can be allocated in a layer of the OSI model.

It can be understood that knowing the OSI model builds a solid foundation to understand all other networking topics in Domain 4. If you know how each attack functions, then you know whether it uses ICMP, TCP, or UDP. This leads to being able to focus on the attacks that are not associated with Layer 4. The exam is not just about memorizing the definition of an attack, but understanding the concept. Do yourself a favor and get to know the OSI Model.

Think Like A Manager

Certain problems need a technical solution. Although not required, it helps if managers have a background in security operations to make more informed decisions.

"SYN" and "Ping" flood are the only choices that directly provide some insight into which layer of the OSI model the attacks occur. To figure that out, you'd have to know the protocols synonymous with using a "SYN" and the protocol used for "Ping". Knowing this can help you confirm which of the choices can be eliminated right away.

Hint: The question is looking for attacks that occur at OSI Layer 3. SYN floods use TCP[1], so now you know it operates at Layer 4. Knowing this eliminates choice B. If you know a Ping flood uses ICMP, which is in Layer 3[2], then you know either choice A or D is correct. This process of elimination has now left only two choices.

To understand how TCP Layer 4 attacks are performed, it is essential to first know the components of a legitimate TCP three-way handshake[3]:
• Client sends SYN segment to server
• Server sends back a SYN/ACK
• Client sends back a corresponding ACK

SYN, SYN-ACK, ACK are the three parts necessary to establish a full TCP connection. One of the benefits of having a full TCP three-way handshake is that it allows data packets to be retransmitted if lost during transmission[4].

Because there isn't a confirmed connection between a client and server when using UDP, data packets do not have an established path to be retransmitted. SMTP, HTTPS, SSH, or FTP are protocols that must have a confirmed connection between a client and server and will use TCP. DHCP, SIP, DNS or TFTP are protocols that do not always require confirmation and use UDP[5].

A. III, IV
B. I, II
C. II, III
D. II, IV

Choice D is the correct answer. Because protections have been put in place for "most" Layer 4 attacks, there is a higher risk of vulnerabilities for Layer 3 attacks. A SYN flood uses Transmission Control Protocol (TCP) and a Fraggle attack uses User Datagram Protocol (UDP)[6], both of which fall under OSI Model Layer 4. A Smurf attack and a Ping flood are under Layer 3, as they both utilize the Internet Control Message Protocol (ICMP)[7].

I. SYN Flood - Layer 4 (TCP)
1. Attacker sends SYN packets toward victim with spoofed source IP
2. Victim server receives SYN, sends SYN/ACK to spoofed source IP
3. Spoofed IP machine drops SYN/ACK, as it never sent an initial SYN
4. Victim server never receives a corresponding ACK[8]

When the victim server accrues a large quantity of unanswered SYN/ACKs, the memory and CPU start to reach an exhausting measure of utilization. At this point, legitimate connections start to get dropped.
Counter-measure: SYN cookies, blackholing, traffic throttling[9]

II. Smurf Attack - Layer 3 (ICMP)
A Smurf attack will use a collection of networked computers to directly flood a victim server with ICMP replies. This is known as an "amplification" attack or a "smurf amplifier". Here is how a Smurf attack works:
1. Attacker spoofs a packet with the source IP address of a victim
2. ICMP Echo Request is sent to a router's broadcast IP address
3. Echo Requests are broadcast to the machines in the network
4. Echo Replies from those machines are then directed to the victim[10]
Counter-measure: Inspect, filter, disable, or block ICMP traffic[11]

III. Fraggle Attack - Layer 4 (UDP)[12]
Here is some good news: if you know how a Smurf attack works then you know how a Fraggle attack works. The key difference is that a Smurf attack uses ICMP and a Fraggle attack uses UDP.
Counter-measure: Filtering or disabling certain UDP services[13]

IV. Ping Flood - Layer 3 (ICMP)[14]
Ping uses ICMP which resides at Layer 3 of the OSI model. The attacker's computer can directly send multiple Echo Request packets toward the victim server, or it can use an amplification process like a Smurf attack. Most modern systems already have counter-measures for SYN and Ping floods.
Counter-measure: Rate-limit or drop ICMP at the network device[15]

Denial-of-Service (DOS) vs Distributed-Denial-of-Service (DDOS)
"Denial of service" is a general term and not a specific type of attack, it is a category of attacks. In a DOS, multiple TCP, UDP, or ICMP packets are generated from a single machine. SYN, Smurf, Fraggle, and Ping flood attacks are all forms of denial of service attacks. They seek to exhaust or crash a system in order to reduce their availability. The more devastating attack used today is the DDOS, where an attacker will use multiple compromised computers (botnet) for a large-scale flood of TCP, UDP, or ICMP packets. Instead of creating their own collection of computers, attackers seek to compromise multiple computers around the world using malware to form their own private botnet[16].
Counter-measure: Content distribution network, load balancing[17]

Core CISSP Concept
BCP/DRP is the high-level countermeasure for denial of service or any other attack geared toward disrupting availability. A documented, maintained, and updated BCP/DRP program gets the business back to normal operations with a minimal loss of downtime and disruption.

Rymar Tech's third-party SaaS cloud vendor has been found with multiple violations of the European Union's General Data Protection Regulation (GDPR). An investigation has discovered that the vendor stores Rymar Tech's cloud data in countries that do not have any mechanism for the enforcement of protecting personal data. The supply chain of different subcontractors who maintain the flow of the SaaS platform have also stored private data on hundreds of their own servers even after the data is no longer useful or relevant. Additionally, the data custodians responsible for media backups and maintenance are capable of viewing the plaintext data at rest. Rymar Tech's senior team wants to continue using the cloud vendor, but the privacy issues must be addressed first. What is the best way to continue using the cloud vendor's services?

A. Implement tokenization
B. Request data encryption
C. Conduct a risk assessment
D. Data obfuscation

Exam Strategy and Mentality

Let's just start by stating the correct answer is C. Sometimes it helps to glance at the correct answer to a practice question before really thinking about it. It provides a reverse perspective and method of reasoning. Here is the concept of why choice C is correct:

Core CISSP Concept

Conduct a risk assessment when engaging, acquiring, merging, or renting the services of not just a cloud service vendor, but any third-party[1].

Understand that the mention of GDPR means Rymar Tech processes the personal information of EU citizens whether they have a business presence in Europe or not.

For the first violation, Article 50 of the GDPR, an independent supervisory authority could have been appointed to work with a third country to promote legislation of personal data protection[2]. The subcontractors also did not follow Article 17, which states the personal data of EU citizens have a right to be forgotten if no longer necessary[3]. The vendor also should have implemented symmetric encryption for the data so unauthorized persons such as the data custodians would not be able to view it when performing their maintenance, per Article 34[4]. If Rymar Tech wants to continue using their cloud services then another risk assessment has to be conducted to readjust for stricter control and protection of privacy. After which, choices A, B, and D could then be requested of the vendor as part of improving their data protection controls to address the existing GDPR issues.

Exam Essentials

Get to know these fairly new security terms: tokenization, pseudonymization, and anonymization.

Tokenization, encryption, and obfuscation sound like similar forms of data hiding techniques, but they have unique methods of functionality. Much like all cryptographic controls, one is not better or worse than the other. It all depends on the value of the data and the amount of effort and cost a company is willing to spend protecting it.

Think Like A Manager

Choice C also conducts due diligence. Choices A, B, and D are examples of due care. Due care is for fixing short-term issues and due diligence is preparing for long-term threats.

A. Implement tokenization

The high-level definition of tokenization is simple: meaningless data that represents meaningful data. It's a way to use a random string of characters to represent actual private data. If a token is disclosed, it provides no value for an attacker[5]. Digital payment service providers use tokens to facilitate purchases at payment terminals using near-field communication[6]. Tokenization differs from encryption in that the value of the token is randomly generated and not mathematically calculated[7]. Tokenization could be a proper control for the SaaS cloud vendor (especially if they are handling digital payments) to implement in order to minimize the exposure of Rymar Tech's private data to other third-parties. However, the decision to use tokenization moving forward would originate from the results of a new risk assessment.

Think Like A Manager

Aside from thinking like a manager, pretend you are a security consultant hired by a corporation. Your job is not to touch anything, but to answer questions and have high-level discussions with management. It would not be about tokenization or encryption, it would be about risk, cost, asset value, or an overall security issue.

B. Request data encryption

In encryption, an algorithm and secret key is used to transform plaintext data into ciphertext[8]. Encryption differs from tokenization in that the encrypted data actually leaves the organization protecting data in motion. In tokenization, the data remains within the organization until referenced by the token. A new token would be required if there is a security failure, data migration, or adherence to changes in compliance or regulatory standards[9].

The SaaS cloud vendor can implement encryption for their supply chain (data in motion) and for their data custodians (data at rest) to uphold confidentiality. Like choices A and D, the request for encryption stems from an assessment to see which cryptographic controls are first lacking and which ones are already in place.

C. Conduct a risk assessment

Conducting a risk assessment would be the best way to continue using the vendor's services. A strong risk management program will have a proactive approach to annually assess a vendor's environment whether there is a security incident or not. The ultimate goal is the alignment of security objectives to the business goals through the prioritization of risks. If irreconcilable issues are found that cannot be mitigated, it will be up to management to decide whether to accept or reject the risk. Following are some questions Rymar Tech could ask their SaaS vendor to address their privacy issues[10]:

- How current are the compliance requirements for GDPR?
- How is data in motion and data at rest kept confidential?
- Do subcontractors or custodians have clearance to view the data?
- What privacy steps are taken when data has to be distributed?
- What are the penalties if contracts or SLAs are not met?
- What are the collection limitations for private data?

Core CISSP Concept

A standard set of risk assessment questions may not work for all environments. Because this question is dealing with GDPR violations, a custom GDPR compliant questionnaire would be practical. The diversity of security requires the examination of methods that elicit meaningful answers.

D. Data obfuscation

Unlike encryption and tokenization, obfuscation is not as complex and merely uses obscurity to mask the data[11]. Obfuscating data can be as simple as re-arranging the letters of a word or converting from ASCII to ANSI format. Obfuscation may not always provide the guaranteed confidentiality of encryption nor does it use a token to represent the original data[12]. The vendor could obfuscate Rymar Tech's data, but it would be less effective than encryption or tokenization. Still, it would only be a request after a risk assessment.

What is the greatest advantage of an IaaS in a private cloud over a public cloud?

A. System granularity
B. Dedicated resources
C. Cost-effective solution
D. Multi-tenant architecture

Exam Strategy and Mentality

Think Like A Manager

Questions which ask for the "greatest", means the correct choice will provide either the best functionality, productivity, security, or value. A manager's job is to balance these services.

The cloud is the next frontier for the security professional. For the CISSP exam and the real world, be prepared to know the following cloud types: public, private, community, and hybrid. Also know the following cloud services: Infrastructure as a Service (IaaS), Platform as a Service (PaaS), and Software as a Service (SaaS). Most importantly, as entire businesses or some of their processes start moving to the cloud, it is the CISSP's job to ensure the security of their data is treated the same as it was within the organization.

Hint: The answer can be found even if you do not know anything about an IaaS. All you have to know is the main difference between a private cloud and a public cloud. Only one choice represents why an organization will specifically go for a private cloud over a public, community, or hybrid cloud.

Knowing about cloud types and cloud service models allows you to ask the following questions, which would help in eliminating some of the choices:

- Is system granularity the greatest advantage in a public or private cloud?
- Which cloud type provides the most dedicated resources without resource pooling[1] with other cloud tenants?
- Which cloud type and service are the most expensive? Although cost should not always be the deciding factor, it all depends on the business requirements.
- Are multi-tenant architectures welcomed or a security concern?

With knowledge of cloud computing terms, the question can then be reworded to adjust for more clarity:

- What is not a reason to get an IaaS in a private cloud?
- What is the least important reason to rent an IaaS in a public cloud?

This may seem like a simple question, but in actuality requires basic knowledge of the common cloud computing terms to answer correctly. It is advised to know your cloud.

Core CISSP Concept

The cloud comes with a price, either on a pay-per-use or charge-per-use basis. Factor in cost, risk, and expectations when choosing a cloud vendor.

The security professional should seek to minimize risk for data in the cloud. It is not that different from the controls implemented for other types of security objectives. The threat of information disclosure, alteration, or destruction still exists. Following are some security considerations for the cloud[2]:

- Structured governance and oversight
- Observance of laws and regulations
- Established trust boundaries
- Hardened cloud architecture
- Authentication and access control
- VM and software isolation
- Data disposal and sanitization
- DOS, outage, and availability protections
- Recognition and response to incidents

These security concerns are for when using the cloud in general, but strongly suggested when using a public cloud because resources and data may flow through shared systems.

A. System granularity
B. Dedicated resources
C. Cost-effective solution
D. Multi-tenant architecture

The greatest advantage of a private cloud for any of its services, not just IaaS, are dedicated resources for a single cloud tenant. A public cloud offers their service to multiple tenants who share resources[3].

Cloud Types[4]

- **Public cloud**
  - A public cloud deployment model has a **multi-tenant architecture**, meaning it provides services to more than one customer and can be used by the general public.
  - **Example:** AWS, Google Cloud, or Microsoft Azure.
- **Private cloud**
  - A private cloud provides **dedicated resources** to a single tenant. It can exist either on- or off-premise. Management of a private cloud can fall on the customer or a third-party.
  - **Example:** A government agency uses an on-premise private cloud behind a firewall to safeguard their critical operations.
- **Community cloud**
  - A community cloud is also a multi-tenant environment like a public cloud, but does not function for everyone. It is for a similar community of organizations.
  - **Example:** Financial organizations sharing a common cloud accounts payable software. Data processing companies accessing a community cloud for data parsing software.
- **Hybrid cloud**
  - A hybrid cloud is a combination of public, private, and community clouds with the workload traversing each cloud type. Interoperability of a technology between multiple infrastructures is a key attribute of hybrid clouds.
  - **Example:** Organizations with an on-site private cloud, off-site public cloud, and an outsourced community cloud.

Cloud Service Models[5]

- **Infrastructure as a Service (IaaS)**
  - With an IaaS, it's like someone handed you just the very basic hardware parts. They handed you a CPU, a RAM stick, a motherboard, a hard drive, or a NIC. But instead of all these components being in your hand to build, it's all virtually presented in the cloud. It is your job to turn on the virtual machines, configure the initial settings, install an operating system (PaaS), and then install the required applications (SaaS). An IaaS provides the most **system granularity** as you are starting at the very bottom level just above the cloud vendor's actual physical hardware.
- **Platform as a Service (PaaS)**
  - Maybe you don't have the budget, training, staff, or knowledge to build an entire network infrastructure.
  - Maybe you just want a "platform" to use Windows Active Directory. Or you want a coding "platform" to code your Python or Java applications. These are the reasons you would get a PaaS.
  - The cloud vendor provides the platform whereas the application and data are provided by the cloud tenant. The security of the platform can be shared by both the tenant and the vendor - it all depends on the service level agreement.
- **Software as a Service (SaaS)**
  - A SaaS provides the ability to rent software or an application instead of paying thousands of dollars to buy it off-the-shelf.
  - Tenants can run the application all day or turn it off to avoid per-hour usage charges, providing cost management.

Core Concept
Just because something is cheaper does not automatically make it a cost-effective solution. A risk analysis will determine if a control, software, system, countermeasure, or vendor is too costly or within budget for the organization.

The IT Department Head (DH) is looking into purchasing a security control for a system that hosts processes owned by the Sales program manager. The system is valued at $5,000,000. The options for the cost of the control are either $2,000,000 from one vendor or $4,000,000 from a different vendor. The IT department initially chooses the $4,000,000 purchase option, but the head of Sales interjects and requests an analysis comparing the two different solutions. After some discussion, both departments decide to go with the $2,000,000 solution.

What role is represented by the head of the Sales department?

A. Data owner
B. System owner
C. Business owner
D. Data processor

Exam Strategy and Mentality

A lot of numbers are thrown around in this question. Does that mean you should immediately start remembering the formulas for single loss expectancy (SLE) or the annual loss expectancy (ALE)? Not always. Remember the CISSP exam is not a math test, it is a test of concepts and managerial thought process. However, it's still important to know the formula for calculating both the SLE and ALE_1:

- SLE = Asset Value x Exposure Factor
- ALE = SLE x ARO

(ARO stands for annualized rate of occurrence)

We are given the asset value of $5,000,000, but not the exposure factor - we will not be able to determine the SLE. Because we cannot determine the SLE, we are unable to determine the ARO. When values are missing, the correct choice will be determined by knowing the concepts.

General questions to ask about each choice:
- A. **Data owner**
  - Who is the data owner? Is anyone in the Sales or IT department a data owner? If so, what "data" do they own?
- B. **System owner**
  - What exactly is a system owner?
  - What is the difference between a data and system owner? Or are they the same entity?
- C. **Business owner**
  - How does the role of business owner differ from a data or system owner?
- D. **Data processor**
  - How come choices A, B, and C end in "owner" and choice D ends in "processor"?

Even without being given the details of the "discussion", which entity would have the ultimate decision about spending money?

Hint: Out of the four choices, the role with "owner" at the end of it is the correct answer. When it comes to financial decisions, the buck stops with someone who has final ownership.

IT wanted to go with the most expensive control, but the head of Sales had a problem with that decision. What could have been the intention to request an analysis of the two prices in order to use the cheaper option? Whatever the reason, think about whether the request of a system owner would supersede a business owner. Does a data owner have any say on purchasing new systems?

Think Like A Manager
If the question does not fully deal with quantitative analysis, cost still should be the main concern. Does the control cost more than the asset? Is money being wasted or saved?

A. Data owner

A data owner is responsible for the information that exists within an organization's ecosystem[2]. They determine the value, criticality, sensitivity, backup, and retention periods. A data owner will typically take care of the classification, labeling, protection, security requirements, and other proper due care of data. Additionally, a data owner should be aware of the following duties and functions[3]:

- Data must align with the mission and business of the organization
- Set a proper policy for the security, control, and sharing of data
- Determine if the data is exclusive or if it can be replaced
- Verify accuracy of the data as well as the retention period
- Confirm if the data can be shared or if it will remain internal
- Data is compliant and has proper intellectual and copyrights
- Conditions surrounding the use of the data are set with all parties

B. System owner

Let's say a network security engineer manages the firewall for Rymar Tech, a company in the middle of a huge project to migrate their database and file servers to a new location. Under the direction of the IT DH, multiple change requests are being issued for both the servers and the firewalls protecting those servers. A security engineer will configure ACLs, VPNs, and NAT among other necessary changes on the firewall. Then a server administrator will make changes on each server such as creating new passwords, updating the operating system, setting RDP access levels, disabling NetBIOS over TCP/IP, or configuring allowable Kerberos encryption types. The changes to the firewall and servers will support the business processes. In this case, the IT DH is the system owner[4]. This person knows how the system works, supports making required security changes on the system, and understands the value the system will provide to support the business.

Exam Essentials

Different books and study guides have various definitions of system owners, as well as NIST 800-18[5]. As with everything CISSP, knowing the exact definition is not necessary, know the general concept.

C. Business owner

Ideally, there should be a compromise between security and cost. IT chose a control that did not cost more than the system itself, but it still was the more expensive control. Perhaps IT saw new and advanced technologies that would better protect their systems. But the business owner may have thought the control picked by IT went overboard or maybe the $4,000,000 control provided more security than necessary. After further analysis, the cheaper option was chosen. Either way, IT still has a control that provides adequate security, and the business owner just saved the company $2,000,000. Bottom line: the role of the business owner grants them the authority to put cost over security if necessary. The business owner cares about maximizing value and profit[6]. IT does not generate profit for the company; information technology actually is an expenditure. The Sales team makes money. Human life is always the #1 priority in an organization, but making money is a close second. Security professionals want the very best technology when protecting business processes. This does not always align with the mindset of a business owner, or the CISSP exam. The best is not always the most cost-effective. The cheaper option was chosen to control cost.

Core CISSP Concept

When SLE, ALE, or ARO calculations start to occur, it means that a risk analysis is now taking place. A risk assessment occurs before an analysis to identify critical assets, their vulnerabilities, and overall value to the business. A risk analysis will then associate this data to a monetary value[7].

D. Data processor

The data processor is a system, agency, or entity that handles the processing of personal data[8]. If the company you work for outsources their payroll service to a third-party, then that third-party is now the data processor. There was no indication of a data processor in this question and this choice could have been immediately eliminated. For the exam, equate the term "data processor" with the GDPR.

The CISO of a global bank is traveling to a country where the Internet is monitored. She needs to send a secret message to the bank's CEO, but her remote VPN client is being blocked by the host nation's Internet service provider. She calls her bank's security officer who suggests to first write up her secret message, hash it with SHA256, encrypt the hash digest with her private key, then email the encrypted hash along with the secret message to the CEO. The CEO will hash the message, decrypt the encrypted hash with the CISO's public key, and compare it to the appended message.
Which of the following has not been achieved?

A. Nonrepudiation
B. Confidentiality
C. Integrity
D. Authentication

Exam Strategy and Mentality

Cryptography provides a high degree of trust that the data we are storing and sending back and forth retains its confidentiality, privacy and integrity.

Core CISSP Concept

Cryptography is strong, but not 100% secure. Time, patience, and the progression of Moore's Law$_1$ will render any encryption or hashing algorithm insecure.

The CISSP is not a cryptology test, however it does require knowing some cryptographic terms to understand what high-level service is provided. For example, the question mentions SHA256, private keys, and a VPN (virtual private network). These are all technical terms, yet the choices are high-level and fundamental data security concepts.

Think Like A Manager

Is it okay that one of the choices has not been achieved? Is the functionality of the other three choices enough for the CISO to send her message securely to the CEO? Are all four a must?

If you have no idea how to even begin answering the question, then try to eliminate which basic cryptographic service has been provided. For example, we know the secret message will be hashed with the SHA256 algorithm. This means at some point the service of integrity has been

provided$_2$, eliminating choice C as the correct answer. Cryptography also provides confidentiality, authentication, and nonrepudiation$_3$, so what still has not been achieved by the CISO? To fully understand the choices, start by learning about asymmetric encryption, public key infrastructure (PKI), hashing algorithms, and how a VPN works. The CISO's objective is to get a secret message to her CEO. If it were not blocked, a remote VPN would have provided confidentiality, integrity, and authentication$_4$. Does that make nonrepudiation the correct answer? No, because nonrepudiation was achieved when the CISO signed the hash with her private key. Digitally signing a message means a sender can never deny sending the message (assuming the sender is always in possession of their private key). This leaves us with either choice B or D. How has confidentiality or authentication not been achieved by the CISO's actions? The security officer's suggestion is not wrong; however, it doesn't go far enough to achieve the full measure of the security considerations that should be taken by the CISO.

Hint: A sender signing a message with their private key provides a different cryptographic service than encrypting the message with a receiver's public key.

A. Nonrepudiation
B. Confidentiality
C. Integrity
D. Authentication

Through the procedures provided by the security officer, the CISO is creating a digital signature. Digital signatures do not provide confidentiality. They provide nonrepudiation, integrity, and authentication[5]. This question tests to see if you knew that choices A and D occur when a message is signed with a private key, and choice B occurs when a message is encrypted with a public key. Both acts of message signing involve asymmetric encryption. Choice C is achieved through hashing.

Asymmetric encryption involves a private and public key[6]. The public key can be shared with anyone, but the private key must never be shared and kept secret at all costs. For asymmetric encryption or PKI to work, both the sender and recipient of a message must have 100% confidence that each one has properly secured and has complete ownership over their private key. Since only the sender signs the hash with their private key in a digital signature, it shows to the recipient that the hash digest can have come only from the sender, they cannot deny sending it (as they should be the only one to have their private key). The inability to deny sending a message is known as **nonrepudiation**[7]. Additionally, signing a message with a private key also shows possession of the private key, proving **authentication**. Hashing the plaintext message with SHA256 will confirm to the recipient that the message did not change in transit, upholding **integrity**[8].

Core CISSP Concept

If you understand the digital signature process, then you start to know a lot about cryptography itself. It can be said that if you understand the concept, usage, and limitations of a digital signature, then you have attained a modest level of knowledge in the entire cryptography domain.

Following is a quick example of the digital signature process:

SENDER'S RESPONSIBILITY[9]
- **Step 1** - Create plaintext message
  - No cryptographic service
- **Step 2** - Hash plaintext message with SHA256
  - The resulting hash digest provides maintenance of **integrity**
- **Step 3** - Sign the resulting hash with private key
  - This provides **nonrepudiation** and **authentication**
- **Step 4** - Send plaintext message and digitally signed hash
  - Appending the plaintext to the signed hash lets the receiver, or anyone else, read and confirm the message has not been changed in transit. There is no confidentiality provided

In order to provide **confidentiality**, the entire digital signature must be encrypted with the receiver's public key[10].

RECEIVER'S RESPONSIBILITY[11]
- **Step 1** - Receive digital signature and plaintext message
  - Receives signed hash and plaintext message
- **Step 2** - Decrypt the signed hash with sender public key
  - Decryption with public key reveals original SHA256 hash
- **Step 3** - Hash plaintext message with SHA256
  - Hash plaintext to compare to the decrypted SHA256 hash
- **Step 4** - Compare decrypted hash with computed hash
  - Message integrity is intact if both hash digests match

A VPN is one of the strongest ways of providing confidentiality for data in motion, but the CISO could not use her VPN client to securely connect to her corporate office. Sending the digital signature and the appended plaintext message via just regular email does not provide confidentiality, the whole message needs to be encrypted. To make sure her message does not succumb to man-in-the-middle attacks, the security officer should have suggested the CISO also encrypt her outgoing emails or any other type of data communication. A digitally signed message provides nonrepudiation, integrity, and authentication. A digitally signed and then encrypted message further provides confidentiality and privacy.

Blue Demolition has experienced an earthquake at their primary facility in Southern California; there was no loss of human life. The hardware within the facility was completely destroyed. Initiating their BCP/DRP, Blue Demolition called in emergency personnel to begin the process of recovering the business operations at their hot site while restoring their primary environment. Critical equipment such as computers, laptops, servers, firewalls, routers, switches, and backup and storage devices were quickly up and running. There was a small delay in getting the network applications up because of the time it took to load up the server data. The company managed to still remain within their maximum tolerable downtime (MTD) and did not breach any service level agreements (SLAs).

Which of the following contributed the least to Blue Demolition's successful BCP/DRP?

A. Delivery time of replacement hardware
B. Standardized assets
C. Policy, scope, and initiation of BCP/DRP program
D. Accurate SLA parameters

Exam Strategy and Mentality

It is important to remember the question is asking for which choice "contributed the least" to a well-executed BCP/DRP.

Exam Essentials

The word "least" means that all the choices are close to being correct, but one choice did not play as important of a role as the other choices. It takes a complete analysis of the question context and the choices to figure out which one is the "least" important.

Hint: The primary site was unavailable but then rapidly made available by a hot site. Which of the choices is most likely not required for this type of site? Did all the choices contribute equally to the BCP/DRP?

What to focus on from the question context:
- There was no loss of human life
- Primary site hardware was destroyed
- Business was recovered at a hot site
- Infrastructure was brought up quickly
- Company remained under MTD
- SLAs were maintained
- Successful BCP/DRP

What to focus on from the choices:
- What needed to be delivered?
- How do standardized assets help?
- Importance of BCP/DRP policy and scope
- Pre-defined SLA parameters
- Which choice may not be necessary at all?

Recovery means to restore critical business functions at the hot site and restoration means to build and repair the damage caused by the earthquake at the primary site[1].

Core CISSP Concept

High-level policies matter more than low-level operations. For the CISSP exam, high-level security objectives must be complete before any of the objectives in security operations. If there is something that is going to be the "least" useful, then it is going to be something that has to do with low-level operations.

Blue Demolition displayed a sense of urgency as they got their infrastructure back up and running within the MTD and without breaking SLAs. They had no time to wait for anything as they were running against the SLA clock. They needed their systems ready to go minutes-to-hours after the natural disaster. Look for the choice that would be a reason for delay.

A. Delivery time of replacement hardware

Looking at the question, what is the primary reason Blue Demolition was able to expediently bring up their critical equipment? It was the use of a hot site. Because it is a hot site, all the equipment was already there just as it would be at the primary site, hardware is not being delivered. What is the difference between a cold, warm, and hot site?

Cold Site[2] A cold site does not contain any of the infrastructure, systems, or software required to bring up the organization right after a disaster. At the least, it will contain the HVAC, plumbing, electrical wiring, and some furniture. Everything else required to bring up the site will have to be delivered at the time of the disaster. Cold sites provide a low-cost solution with the longest recovery time.

Warm Site[3] Associate the word "partial" when thinking of a warm site; everything is partially ready. Routers, switches, firewalls, or servers may be ready, they just need to be physically connected. The initial network connectivity may need to be set up. Server images, ISOs, or data may still need to be delivered to the site. Warm sites provide a medium-cost solution with a medium-length recovery time.

Hot Site[4] For a company that requires a fully operational site with critical networking hardware, server software, and capacity considerations ready to go immediately or within a few short hours, regardless of the cost, hot sites are the solution. Depending on their BCP/DRP planning, data may already be at the hot site via backups, remote journaling, or electronic vaulting. This type of assurance comes with a heavy cost as hot sites are the most expensive solution with the shortest recovery time.

Think Like A Manager

It is during the business impact analysis (BIA) in which the values for MTD, RTO, RPO for critical assets are calculated[5]. Additionally, the decision to have a cold, warm, or hot site is determined during the recovery strategies phase of the organization's BCP/DRP.

B. Standardized assets

The standardization of assets can provide the confidence necessary for a smooth BCP/DRP process. Imagine your organization experiences a total disaster, transfers to a warm site, then realizes that the disaster recovery team brought over copies of Windows when the recovery site only has machines available for Linux distributions. This considerable difference can make or break an organization's maximum tolerable downtime during BCP/DRP. It is important to make sure the equipment used at the primary business site matches that of the recovery site. For maximum efficiency, standards should be mandatory[6].

C. Policy, scope, and initiation of BCP/DRP program

You must absolutely have a policy in place to not only begin a BCP/DRP plan but to also even have a BCP/DRP program. A policy is issued by senior management and nothing gets done without their support and directive. Phase 1 of BCP/DRP planning also includes the scope, which means to define the who, what, when, and where of the BCP/DRP program. Having scope reduces wasting time and spending money on actions that do not directly contribute to the BCP/DRP[7]. Scope keeps people, processes, and responsibilities within a specific and narrow path. Finally, without the initiation of a BCP/DRP program, there would not be a program at all. We can talk all about policy and scope, but someone has to take the initiative to start the BCP/DRP program.

D. Accurate SLA parameters

Defining a service level agreement between a customer and a vendor has multiple benefits. First, a well-written SLA can prevent unexpected disruptions or delays during a disaster. Second, it can serve to put an official mean time to recovery (MTTR) for a failed asset[8]. Third, if an organization is going to transfer the risk of an asset, an SLA forces the organization to perform a risk analysis to determine their most valuable assets. As in, if they're paying a vendor to protect an asset, it's going to be one that is valuable.

You are tasked with designing Rymar Tech's firewall architecture. The following three requirements must be met per senior management: at least two firewalls have to be deployed for two different subnets, a demilitarized zone (DMZ) is required, and a design must be created that provides the least amount of administrative overhead for security operations.

Which type of firewall deployment architecture will you choose?

A. Two-tier I
B. Two-tier II
C. Three-tier I
D. Three-tier II

Exam Strategy and Mentality

This is a straight technical question. There is not a high-level aspect to it, you just have to know the technical aspects of firewall deployment architectures. Let's take a look at the requirements again to see if we can narrow the best possible choice by process of elimination.

At Least Two Firewalls

Management requires the new architecture to have "at least two firewalls". To get this question correct, you have to know how many firewalls are utilized in each type of deployment. The choices do not translate to the number of firewalls, as in two-tier does not mean there are two firewalls and three-tier does not mean there are three firewalls. You cannot eliminate choice C and D right away just because it has the word "three". If you have no idea at all, just guess, as leaving an answer blank is considered incorrect on the exam. Note that the two firewalls are to be separate, not in high-availability.

DMZ is Required

Since a DMZ is "required", it means at least three choices contain a DMZ network. If all choices contain a DMZ, then it's a matter of looking at which of the other requirements are missing. DMZs are traditionally separated from the internal network, so even a single firewall architecture will be able to have multiple networks. Firewalls traditionally contain multiple interfaces for segmenting multiple networks.

Least Administrative Overhead

Choice D, a three-tier II deployment just sounds like it would be a complex design and deserving of the most commitment of administrative man-

agement. "Tier" is the major term to understand. Tier refers to the number of protected networks or subnets. Three-tier firewalls have three networks and two-tier firewalls have two networks[1]. Knowing the difference between the two will help you get this question correct. In this sense, both choices C and D may be eliminated.

Exam Essentials

Different terminology exists for firewalls and networking. For the exam, stick with the terms in the official guides.

With the pen and paper provided at the testing center, quickly sketch out what an architecture with two firewalls protecting a DMZ and a private network would look like. Chances are you will draw the one with the least administrative overhead first.

Core CISSP Concept

Firewalls are one of the most important network security devices. A security professional and someone who wants to become a CISSP, with firewall experience or not, has to know a little bit about them. Get to know the difference between a packet filter and stateful filtering firewall or that firewalls are OSI Model Layer 3 networking devices.

A. Two-tier I

In this setup a single firewall is protecting two separate networks. The traffic comes in from the Internet, hits the router, and depending on the destination address, the firewall will then send it toward the DMZ network or toward the private network[2]. Two-tier I firewalls use at least three network interfaces and can separate two or more networks. The physical interfaces on a firewall or router can each be assigned to different networks with copper or fiber optic cables[3].

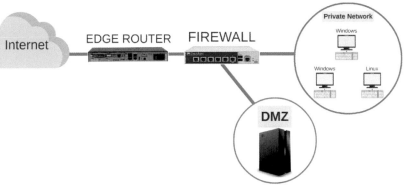

While this architecture has a DMZ and is easier to manage than the other choices, it consists of only one deployed firewall.

B. Two-tier II

Two-tier II deployments practice defense-in-depth, as it requires two firewalls to inspect traffic inbound to the private network[4]. A DMZ exists inline and is protected by the first firewall. This deployment requires increased routing and access-control rules.

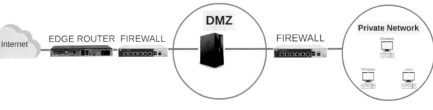

Choice B meets the requirements of at least two firewalls, a DMZ, and of all the other choices, has the least administrative complexity.

C. Three-tier I

Three-tier systems can be the most secure as traffic is filtered from subnet-to-subnet until reaching the private network. Three-tier I deployments consist of three firewalls[5]. A single routing change on the network may require updated routes and ACLs on all three firewalls, making them the most complex architecture to manage.

Neither of the three-tier deployments would meet the requirements.

D. Three-tier II

This matches the two-tier II deployment in terms of the DMZ and number of firewalls used, but this design also creates a transaction subnet between the two firewalls that must be managed[6].

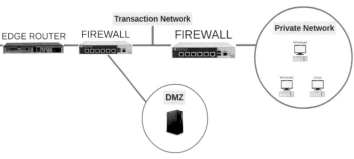

The transaction subnet creates an added layer of administrative complexity just like with three-tier I deployments.

Core CISSP Concept

Firewall architecture concepts are the same, but they do not always fit every organization. When choosing a firewall deployment architecture consider the cost, overhead, complexity, and most importantly, the value of the asset it is protecting.

A breach of user information occurred at Rymar Tech when a human resources employee was able to download private data to a USB drive and walk out the front door. It has prompted a government investigation that could result in a $50 million fine. The results of the investigation showed that even though security administrators followed a policy to prevent personal USB drives from being used on corporate machines, the employee used a company-issued storage device. Even though the employee had the necessary experience and cleared a thorough background check before employment, the employee failed to mention she briefly worked for a competitor's firm. Even though security guards, CCTVs, a mantrap, and a badge reader were implemented at the front entrance, there was no way to detect the USB drive in the employee's back pocket.

The investigation concluded with Rymar Tech's fine reduced to $10 million. Moving forward, it was suggested they implement a stronger data loss prevention control as well as a more stringent hiring process to lessen the risk of this kind of incident in the future. Which of the following is the best reason the fine was reduced?

A. Compliance
B. Due diligence
C. Due care
D. Risk assessments

Exam Strategy and Mentality

The CISSP is not about getting into the real specifics of a topic. Think about who is involved in this situation? What were their responsibilities? Did anyone fail to do their job? Did Rymar Tech do everything in their power to control this type of risk?

If not, what would lessen the risk of this type of incident from happening again? Would any other types of laws have been broken if Rymar Tech's security guards tried to physically stop and search the employee?

Think Like A Manager

Senior management must be aware of the risks to their organization from all vectors. This can be achieved through a multi-level and comprehensive risk management framework that includes the categorization, selection, implementation, assessment, authorization, and continual monitoring of risk[1]. The success or failure to prudently address risk factors is a reflection of company leadership. Risk-aware leadership instills confidence and can shape an employee's own security awareness mindset.

Exam Essentials

The "best" choice requires applying deep-level CISSP concepts. The answer cannot be looked up in a book.

Security breaches have become serious business as they can lead to fines, firings, class-action lawsuits[2], and business closures.

Hint: Here is the secret to getting this question correct: know the difference between due care and due diligence. Think of which one will be scrutinized in an investigation from a legal standpoint.

A. Compliance

Privacy and the right to privacy has brought the creation of multiple laws and regulations in order to better protect private information. The GDPR, PCI DSS, and PIPEDA are forms of privacy protection laws aimed at making sure organizations are doing their due care to keep user information safe[3]. Failure to follow compliance can result in legal action that could incur multiple fines and penalties[4]. Making sure to understand compliance requirements is a part of the due diligence process, while implementing the controls to uphold compliance would be due care. Rymar Tech was not following any particular compliance, nor is it a reason to reduce fines if followed.

B. Due diligence

Conducting due diligence falls on the responsibility of those in senior management. It is the act of due diligence that results in the actions of due care; for without due diligence there is no due care[5]. Disabling personal USB drives on corporate computers (technical), conducting background checks (administrative), having security guards, CCTVs, and badge readers (physical) are examples of due care security controls. These controls only exist as a result of policies created by a wider risk-focused research program initiated by management.

Think Like A Manager

Due diligence is a methodical approach to choosing and customizing appropriate risk-based due care security controls that uphold the company's goals, responsibilities, processes, applications, assets, and above all, human life.

The due diligence done before the breach is proactive, while due diligence after the breach is reactive. Reactive due diligence is about understanding the reason behind an incident, event, or breach and making sure the steps to rectify the situation are done within measured risk parameters. Whether it is mandated from within the company or under legal action, due diligence has the primary responsibility of making sure the same incident does not occur twice.

Core CISSP Concept

Due diligence and due care are simply ways to show that the company cares about their risks. There is never a way to eliminate all risk, which means there is always some level of risk. Due diligence shows prudent executive leadership and due care shows judicious security operations.

C. Due care

A lack of assigned due care controls by executives can lead to legal action[6]. For Rymar Tech, the fines were reduced because they had in place adequate technical, administrative, and physical due care security controls. Despite the insider attack being able to circumvent the controls, the company was proactive in their approach to risk management. It takes due diligence to make sure all these due care measures are in place and continuously maintained. Essentially, Rymar Tech did everything they could to mitigate their risk of a data breach, just short of a full body search. They were not able to completely eliminate this risk. Moving forward, a policy limiting employee privacy in the workplace could provide a pathway to search personal employee property, including emptying out pockets.

Due diligence is performed by senior management and comes before due care. Diligence is about knowing and due care is about doing.

D. Risk assessments

Conducting proper risk assessments throughout the organization at least once a year is a part of performing due diligence. The results of a risk assessment are the formal way to determine due care controls.

Exam Essentials

Sometimes due care is an action that should most likely be taken, and due diligence is an action that may not be necessary, but is best for the long-term.

Rymar Tech is conducting a quantitative analysis of their financial file server. The SLE for the server is $50,000. The organization wants to account for the file server to fail once every two years. Three different managers have provided their suggestions for the necessary security controls required to protect the file server from a potential breach, denial of service, or other types of compromise.

Manager 1 has suggested putting in two $3,000 firewalls in an active/standby pair. Manager 2 wants to place a state-of-the-art biometric device in front of the server room. Right now, only authorized employees of Rymar Tech are allowed to enter the room by swiping a badge and entering a PIN. The new device would replace the badge and PIN system and only authorized employees would go through the initial biometric enrollment phase. In addition to the high-availability firewalls, Manager 3 wants to also install an intrusion prevention system, an intrusion detection system, a load balancer, and purchase a hot site with data from the original file server being replicated via remote journaling.

Which manager has provided the most effective choice?

A. Manager 1
B. Manager 2
C. Manager 3
D. Manager 1 & 3

Exam Strategy and Mentality

At its core, this question is the embodiment of thinking like a manager. Three managers have provided three different suggestions and it is your job to take all that you have learned in your CISSP journey and choose the "most effective" choice. All of the choices may seem correct, but one choice does not have any unnecessary controls that affect cost, security, or network design.

Hint: It is best to calculate the value of the asset first and then compare it to the cost of the suggested controls.

Exam Essentials

Study the technical terms and concepts in order to understand the question, not to answer it.

Think of the CISSP as a business exam with technical terminology. We study risk, disaster recovery, processes, frameworks, access control, software life cycles, dynamic routing, and other elements of network security operations. All this knowledge goes into evaluating the question to see which choices affect the cost, revenue, and expansion of a business.

Think Like A Manager

A percentage of uncertainty always exists with asset calculations. A confidence level should be considered whenever taking into account the breakdown of an ALE_1.

Manager 1 suggests spending $6,000 total on two firewalls. Manager 2 wants a new biometric access control system. Manager 3 wants to add more network security devices. If you can't understand the question, think instead of which choice ultimately reduces the risk to the three cornerstone concepts of confidentiality, integrity, or availability.

A. Manager 1

Right away the question requires calculating the annual loss expectancy of the file server. This is done through multiplying the single loss expectancy (SLE) by the annualized rate of occurrence (ARO)[2]. The SLE is given in the question as $50,000. The ARO is .5, since Rymar Tech expects the file server to "fail once every two years". The ALE is $25,000.

$$\underline{SLE \times ARO = ALE}$$
$$\$50,000 \times .5 = \$25,000$$

If the value of the file server is $50,000, and it fails once every two years, then the annual loss will be $25,000.

Core CISSP Concept

The cost of the security control should not exceed the asset[3]. You don't want to protect a $50,000 file server with an $80,000 firewall. If the control costs more than the asset, management may decide to forgo the control and accept the risk.

Manager 1 has suggested a $3,000 firewall in high-availability mode, which means two firewalls are required for a total of $6,000. High-availability means to deploy two firewalls, one being the active firewall protecting the network, and the other a standby firewall in case the active one fails (both can also be in active/active mode)[4]. High-availability prevents a single point of failure[5]. If the file server were to fail once in two years, it would cost the company $25,000. Purchasing a technical preventative control that costs a total of $6,000 would be a cost-effective measure. A high-availability firewall pair would be an adequate control to prevent unauthorized access to the file server from external threats in an effort to preserve confidentiality and integrity. If a threat brings down the primary firewall, the secondary is there to take over, upholding availability. Manager 1 has suggested the most effective solution.

B. Manager 2

When a badge and PIN are used for gaining access to an asset, two-factor authentication is taking place[6]. By removing the use of a badge and a PIN, Manager 2 has actually made access to the file server less secure, as two-factor authentication is more secure than single-factor authentication any day of the week. If a biometric system replaced both these two forms of authentication, it would be using single-factor authentication. As technologically accurate as it may be, a biometric system by itself is just proving something you are. Entering biometric information coupled with something you have (badge) or something you know (PIN) would work better to uphold confidentiality and integrity. From a manager's perspective, biometric devices are an expensive cost. It costs money not just to buy it, but to hire the professionals who need to administer the system, enroll users, generate templates, balance the crossover error rate, and provide continuous administrative support[7]. Ultimately, Manager 2's suggestion is not the most effective choice because it increases cost and lessens the security posture of the organization.

C. Manager 3

Manager 3's suggestion is not correct due to: the addition of a load balancer. A load balancer is meant to mathematically distribute network traffic proportionally across multiple servers or network devices[8]. The question focuses only on one financial file server. There is not another server to distribute the traffic load coming into the network; a load balancer is not necessary. The cost of an additional IPS, IDS, load balancer, and hot site were not mentioned and they all combined could have been more or less than the cost of the file server itself, but that was not the determining factor. However, all the additional devices sans the load balancer could provide adequate security for the file server depending on cost.

D. Manager 1 & 3

Only Manager 1's suggestion is correct.

A security operations center (SOC) has lost three firewall engineers and does not have the budget to hire replacements. Management has given Casey, the service desk technician, the additional responsibility of only viewing firewall configurations for customer tickets. She is to make sure the right firewall policies, VPN usernames, and network address translation rules exist on the firewall, as well as verifying if site-to-site IPSec tunnels are active. The security administrator has created an account for Casey that enables her to view the firewall configuration and deploy any necessary changes as long as it is approved by a senior engineer.

Which form of access management has not been followed?

A. Need to know
B. Least privilege
C. Job rotation
D. Separation of duties

Exam Strategy and Mentality

In addition to service desk tasks, Casey is now being asked to take on more technical responsibilities. When this happens in a company, it is up to the security professional to make sure access is properly provisioned. While Casey may currently be in a role that limits her network device access, the addition of her new firewall responsibilities now increases those rights and privileges. This in turn can be a direct correlation to the SOC's overall risk exposure[1]. If Casey was leaving her old role for a new one, it would be best practice to remove her previous access.

Authorization creep will occur if a worker's rights and permissions have not been removed when rotating to new job positions[2]. In the question though, she is receiving more rights in addition to her existing ones.

Casey's current role deals with service desk tasks and not firewall issues. She would not have as much experience in her new technical role as the previous SOC engineers. This can lead to mistakes and has to be accounted for when considering what level of access to provide Casey. In this regard, the systems administrator has given her read access as well as write access, but only with prior approval. This follows a proper change management process in security operations.

Change management steps include the request, approval, testing, implementation, and documentation of all firewall configuration changes regardless of skill level[3]. It is a way to make sure firewall engineers can't just make any changes they want to a firewall; it limits their power over critical operations. Change management also is a way to catch mistakes before they are implemented on the firewall.

Casey's new role will require an additional level of need to know access. Least privilege will then further restrict that access to just the tasks related to her job. Presently, Casey has not only need to know access to perform her job as a service desk technician, but will also require read-only access to the firewalls.

In due time, when more engineers have been hired, Casey's firewall rights and privileges will have to be revoked. The glaring security flaw that has not been followed will stand out to two types of people: security professionals with years of experience or those who have thoroughly understood their CISSP concepts. There is no experience requirement to take the CISSP exam, but it is highly recommended. Spending time understanding concepts, whether at work or at home, is the only way to gain security knowledge and to accumulate the wisdom to fix broken processes.

A. Need to know

Giving only the access required to do the job is practicing proper need to know[4]. The goal of implementing need to know is to prevent unapproved access. This was followed when management gave Casey need to know access to customer firewalls in order to accommodate her new job role. However, she is supposed to be only "viewing" and "verifying" the configurations, as management did not state she is to make any kind of changes to the firewall. The security administrator fulfilled Casey's need to know by creating a firewall account to view the configuration, but violated the directive by also allowing Casey to deploy changes. This is not the correct choice because Casey was given need to know access to the firewall, but her least privilege was not restricted to just read operations.

B. Least privilege

By allowing Casey to have write access to the firewall as well as read-only access, the security administrator failed to follow the principle of least privilege. Least privilege will fine-tune a subject's access to an object by assigning just the very minimum rights and permissions to it[5]. Casey required need to know access to the firewall with management's permission to read configurations only, not the additional privilege to make actual changes.

Since senior management is ultimately responsible for what happens in an organization, they should be careful when deciding which roles get what level of access. Need to know and least privilege are collaborative controls to protect confidentiality and integrity by confining a user's access just to their job role. They prevent a user from making a mistake on systems outside of their scope. It can also limit what an attacker can access in case of an account compromise[6].

Core CISSP Concept

Utilize need to know with the addition of least privilege in order to restrict users to the very minimum access required to perform their jobs. Then enforce job rotation and separation of duties to uncover fraud, collusion, or an abuse of position by those with low or high-risk privileges.

C. Job rotation

One of the primary reasons to enforce job rotation is to uncover or minimize the acts of collusion and fraud[7]. If a user knows that someone else will come in and perform their job for a while, they are less likely to commit a crime. While job rotation may commonly mean a previous position was relinquished, in Casey's circumstance she was temporarily rotated to an engineering role while also maintaining her service desk role. This goes along with the secondary reasons for job rotation: backup for employee shortages, preparation for a succession plan, and improvement of skills.

Think Like A Manager

A job rotation policy requires the application of the principles of need to know and least privilege. Whether juggling multiple roles or a single new duty, managers must consistently check any accrued rights and permissions a user no longer needs to perform the job. If privilege creep occurs, those rights must be removed.

D. Separation of duties

Separation of duties prevents a single person from performing a high-impact task[8]. A single firewall engineer who can request, design, and implement changes to a firewall by themselves and without permission, has a significant degree of power. They can collude with outside entities to give them unfettered access to the protected network behind the firewall, or the firewall itself. Even if a security professional remains virtuous, a compromise of their own account would lead to the attacker now having the same access. Even though it was a mistake for the security administrator to give Casey write access to the firewall, separation of duties still was followed as all changes had to be first approved by a senior engineer.

Exam Essentials

Need to know, least privilege, and separation of duties are preventative controls[9]. Job rotation is a detective control[10] (meant to uncover, not prevent). All four choices fall under administrative controls.

Expenses, extra responsibilities, and reduced profits are a result of what?

A. Security

B. Efficiency

C. Convenience

D. Operability

Exam Strategy and Mentality

Only one of the choices will result in all three of the outcomes presented in this question. Ideally, a business would like to attain all four of the choices: maximum security, high efficiency, ultra-convenience, and smooth operability. Each of the choices has its own strengths and weaknesses.

Security

Think of how security is perceived during our CISSP exam studies. Is security a negative or positive addition to an organization? Does a business actively seek out security? Does it look to security to lower expenses, reduce responsibilities, or increase profits? Would security be an obstacle, necessity, or a cost which contributes to or reduces these effects? Emotionally, think of how you and your fellow security professionals feel about security as compared to your senior management team.

Think Like A Manager

Answer the above questions not as a technical professional, but as a business-driven executive. Costs, an increase in workload, and lower profits all are a manager's nightmare.

Efficiency

High efficiency - that is a manager's dream. Efficiency for a business means to squeeze every bit of work out of daily tasks in order to further focus on more complex problems. Developers want to focus on building new software, not to keep patching and updating old software. Network engineers want to fine-tune the organization's bandwidth usage, not continuously troubleshoot connectivity issues. By increasing efficiency, we also are increasing the effectiveness of measured security controls. Would this result in any of the outcomes in the question?

Convenience

Security professionals and business executives may not consider convenience to be one of their top priorities, yet it absolutely must be. Not everyone in a company may be highly technical or aware of security in their role, so some require a modest level of convenience to perform their job. When employees can perform their job, productivity goes up. We can say that convenience can increase productivity, which will increase profits. As a CISSP, we must provide a balance between security and user convenience. For example, two-factor authentication is useless if a user does not know how to correctly use it.

Operability

Operability can be likened to reliability in that there is a high degree of confidence that something will work from start to finish. A security professional may practice a "security" mindset at their organization, but if that same security professional were to go skydiving, they would want the parachute to have greater operability instead of a high level of security. In an enterprise, operability and security must be balanced to provide something that works as it is supposed to and with the least amount of risk while doing so. When it comes down to it, is operability expected to increase expenses or revenue for the company? Will it add more work to maintain a certain level of operability? Will it cut into the bottom line?

The CISSP is as much a security exam as it is an understanding of the industry's lexicon. Gaining insight into the language of the CISSP helps to answer the questions in the same frame of mind. The only way to learn a new language is to immerse yourself in it. Incorporate the same terms, definitions, and vocabulary learned in your books to your own real-life situations. It is also easier to study this exam if you surround yourself with those on the same mission as you.

A. Security

To profit-driven businesses, information security is an after-thought. To software development, security is an impediment to innovation. To financial exchanges, security slows down commerce. To the business leaders of an organization, security can be just another thing they have to do in order to maintain compliance. In other words, security is just another cost, an inconvenience to productivity, and a roadblock to revenue growth. Security just now is becoming important not only for the safety of information but also human lives.

It takes the security professional a full understanding of the policies, functions, processes, and culture of the organization to make security part of its DNA. The introduction of a security program adds cost, new responsibilities, and takes away from profit. Firewalls, anti-virus software, and biometric systems are expenses for companies that did not need them before. It forces them to create new job roles such as network security engineers, systems administrators, or physical security guards. Money that otherwise could have been considered profit is now being diverted to the security program. Security is not here to make money, it is a cost that helps to reduce, avoid, accept, or transfer risk.

Core CISSP Concept

Overall business goals are to lower expenses, reduce overhead, and increase profits while maintaining a balance between confidentiality, integrity, and availability of services. A cost-effective, scalable, and managed information security and risk management program helps achieve these goals.

Efficiency, convenience, and operability are welcomed in an organization as they can be expected to yield positive and quantifiable results. Security does not play a hand in generating revenue or bringing potential sales. In security, we spend a lot of money on protections and pay people a lot of money to do it. We do this hoping to avoid a data breach incident, system outages, or the watchful specter of regulatory non-compliance.

Think Like A Manager

A manager will try to use the security program itself to not only protect company assets, but also attempt to produce measurable cost-saving results[1]. One of the ways to do this is to first understand the business objectives and find reflective security controls[2].

B. Efficiency

Peak efficiency and effectiveness of programs and systems occur if they are operating as intended, have correctly implemented security controls, and are meeting desired outcomes[3]. If an intrusion prevention system (IPS) is blocking network traffic containing malicious signatures, it is operating as intended. Security controls such as frequent IPS signature updates, restrictive access control, and high-availability add to its desired effectiveness in reducing the total amount of security incidents. Expenses are lowered, additional responsibilities are not necessary, and profits are increased when a company does not have to deal with frequent security events.

C. Convenience

Security is not here to be convenient, but security and convenience have to play nice with each other. If users find memorizing long and complex passwords too inconvenient, they will write it down on a piece of paper. To provide both convenience and security, the security advisor can suggest using passphrases, as they are easier to remember while satisfying password complexity requirements.

D. Operability

The CISSP is an exam for security professionals, but it also takes a business executive's frame of mind to succeed. Both want a secure and operational system, but given a choice, operability drives the business. At the same time, operability needs the functions of security to prevent or lessen its own downtime. Operability is not an added expense with extra responsibilities that cuts into the profit margin; operability is mandatory. The result of operability is a functioning business continuing to be fully engaged in cutting cost, reducing overhead, and focusing on profits.

Fred has been contracted as a penetration tester. He will have access to the internal lines of code and general design of an application that needs to be tested. Fred always has had malicious intent. Howard is testing the same software without any prior knowledge. He will approach his duty as if thinking like a malicious attacker. Howard is a security professional.

Robin is an ethical hacker who has been tasked to cover the vulnerabilities missed by Fred and Howard. She has been given some information about a system, but not everything. Gary is performing SQL injections in a test environment. He has created a database and is now testing it for vulnerabilities. Gary is a programmer.

Who can do the most damage?

A. Fred
B. Howard
C. Robin
D. Gary

Exam Strategy and Mentality

Think of which individual would cause the least damage to eliminate a choice right away. Look for the type of testing that would be the most isolated away from a production environment. Then look for which individual would have the least motivation or tendency to cause intentional damage. This can be determined by their skill level and knowledge of the weaknesses in the system. Just because someone has been hired by a company does not always mean they will be ethical during or after they have completed their assignment.

Hint: The context of the question gives insight into the background and the extent of each individual's knowledge.

Think Like A Manager

System testing should not be just a one-time occurrence. As new vulnerabilities develop over time, it is important to remain vigilant by perpetually testing new and older systems[1].

The criticality of a system determines the frequency of testing[2]. For example, systems with a low maximum tolerable downtime (MTD) should be tested as much as possible if not continuously. Infrequent or annual testing can be performed on systems with a high MTD that would not cause damage to the business if unavailable. An MTD sets the approximate time sensitivity associated with recovering a business function[3]. A low MTD could be between two to four hours and a high MTD could be seven to 14 days.

Factors such as scope, level of access, and total knowledge of the system determines the type of testing required. One type of test does not work for every company and it is advised to use multiple types to get a holistic view. Likewise, not all systems are alike and each one requires a different testing tool.

To maximize the coverage of unseen areas of a system, use both automated and manual testing tools[4]. Penetration testing is not only about attacking a target system, but also a test of the company's own ability to respond and defend against attack. Although damage can disrupt business operations, the information gained from the incident can be more beneficial in the company's long-term security[5]. An organization's security program can only evolve if it can prevent the same incident from frequent occurrence.

A. Fred

Fred is performing white box testing. This kind of test provides him detailed information on the internal workings of software and the lines of code before any kind of test is even conducted[6]. White box testing helps target a specific area of software vulnerabilities for a more comprehensive result. The fact that Fred knows all about the software before testing it, provides him the knowledge to perform penetration tests from multiple known vectors. In other words, Fred does not have to do any kind of reconnaissance on the target to find vulnerabilities. Out of all the types of testing, white box testing provides the most cost-effective technique[7], however, someone having full knowledge before conducting an external attack is not realistic of actual real-world threats. It takes black box testing to understand all the possible and unseen ways an adversary will try to compromise a system.

Fred can leverage his position as a contractor with authorized access to do the most damage as an insider threat. He also could cause the most damage if he left the company, as he would be taking the knowledge with him. Apart from just damage, Fred could also steal, sabotage, or sell the information to a competitor.

RFC 1918 IP networks, physical environments, or remote access connections are some common insider threat vectors and it is suggested a combination of detection, prevention, and deterrence controls exist to cover each point[8]. In addition to controls, security training and awareness improve user recognition of malicious activities[9]. Security knowledge improves the ability to use a system while also lessening the chances of making mistakes on it.

Think Like A Manager

A way to mitigate internal threats is to establish a solid baseline of expected behavior, personalities, network traffic, and access of all users[10]. These general characteristics will better measure internal users who are going outside the boundaries of normal activity.

B. Howard

Howard is performing black box testing. Because he is approaching the system with zero knowledge of how it works or functions, black box testing can provide results most reflective of the real world[11]. The insight gained from this type of test not only helps discover new threat vectors, but also prioritize risks and remediate them in order of importance. Howard is conducting black box testing in a professional capacity. It should be cautioned that black box testing also gives Howard the chance to inadvertently affect parts of the system beyond the scope of the test. Without any prior knowledge of the internal workings of the system, Howard also may fail to fully test the controls that actually need to be tested[12]. If there was any damage, it would most likely come from making mistakes or unintentionally affecting interdependent systems. Either way, by giving permission to conduct black box security testing, the organization has accepted the risk of potential damage.

C. Robin

Robin is performing gray box testing, which can be used to patch the spots missed by both black and white box testing[13]. Gray box testing makes up for the internal controls missed by black box testing and provides an added element of realism missing in white box testing. Any damage caused by Robin is either unintentional or done so in a controlled manner. As an ethical hacker, Robin has already obtained management's acceptance to expect this kind of damage.

D. Gary

Gary would cause the least amount of damage because SQL injections performed on his database will never leave the confines of his lab.

Core CISSP Concept

Penetration testing is a craft that requires great skill, planning, communication, and documentation. While sometimes systems may be damaged during a test, this action itself is a learning opportunity beneficial to understanding how it can be prevented next time.

QUESTION 20

At which phase of the software development life cycle (SDLC) should security be implemented first?

A. Initiation
B. Development/Acquisition

C. Implementation/Assessment
D. Operations and Maintenance

Exam Strategy and Mentality

Software developers and security professionals have two different objectives. Developers are about creating a quality product with a certain aspect of appeal and functionality. Security professionals reduce threats to the product while also protecting other systems from the product. Which choice would play the most deep-rooted and continual role in the long-term if it were to have security first? Removing vulnerabilities at this phase first also provides the most long-term cost savings.

Think Like A Manager
Releasing frequent patches, hotfixes, or updates after the deployment of software may wind up costing more had the security flaws been fixed during initial development.

The following defenses can be formed as a protective perimeter around software: host-based intrusion detection systems, firewalls, IPS/IDS devices, hard disk encryption, or SSL inspection. At a high-level, would the purchase of all these controls be necessary if vulnerabilities were eliminated during software development?

Security can be implemented during the **initiation** phase of the SDLC just by the mention of its existence. While everyone else is talking about business functionality and goals, the security professional has to carefully place emphasis on the right type of security to uphold those same business objectives[1]. As discussions about money and operability take the lead, someone has to interject with addressing security. The security and business objective discussion can then be further formalized into a baseline during the **development or acquisition** phase[2]. Security is important in this phase as it is focused not only on the system itself, but also the effect it will have on other systems once system integration has been completed. This also is the time to look into supply chain risks if acquiring a system instead of developing it[3].

Once the system has been **implemented** into a production environment, more security testing and **assessments** are required to complete the certification and accreditation of the system[4]. Once fully **operational**, it is important to **maintain** a rigid change management process[5]. This ensures that any system changes will be reviewed before implementation as to avoid unforeseen security implications.

Think Like A Manager
Even minimal security early on in any of the phases provide developers the ability to detect risks early, adding value to the system and lowering the total cost of ownership.

Think about where planting the idea of security would have the highest impact on the current and future value of the system. Is it better to start security from the very beginning or is it unnecessary to use up resources at this early phase when it could be focused on the product functionality instead? Should security be implemented when the actual development is occurring, when the actual architecture and coding is being done, or should security start when the system is being implemented into a live operational network? After all, if at this point the new system manages to inadvertently stop other critical business functions, the whole project may have to be scrapped anyway. The decision of when to initiate security will have a cascading effect in all the other phases of the SDLC. The true measure of the security considerations during software development life cycle will be revealed if the software ever falls under the publicly known Common Vulnerabilities and Exposure (CVE) list[6].

A. Initiation

The first place to start security planning is the initial phase of the $SDLC_7$. At a high-level, this phase has the most management-facing exposure, thereby having the most influence in their decisions. The initial phase includes assessing the software's impact on the current business functions along with an ideal measure of the recovery point and time objectives$_8$. This phase enforces security beyond just system information, but also the risks to private user data when at rest, stored, or in use. This is the phase when an SDLC model is chosen for the developers to follow. Software development models are not followed as accurately as depicted in our CISSP study guides. It depends on the company environment and whether they want to choose a standard model or one which is security-centric$_9$.

Core CISSP Concept

A secure development task first starts with an accurate concept of the software's operations. This is followed by a set of standards, processes, assessments, quality assurance, secure coding practices, and security training for the entire software development team$_{10}$.

After identifying the security requirements, assessing risk, and performing a privacy impact assessment of the software, it then comes down to the following questions$_{11}$:

- Does the software present a convincing business case?
- Is the cost/benefit ratio showing long-term value and ROI?
- Are there efforts to minimize risk to an acceptable level?
- Will management accept the risks?
- Will it align security with operational efficiency and convenience?
- Is there a wholly planned development life-cycle strategy?

Exam Essentials

Besides the SDLC, the initiation phase of any other process should have security from the beginning. These include BCP/DRP, PKI, IoT, mobile security, chain of custody, or governance and compliance.

B. Development/Acquisition

Users and system experts work together in this stage to turn the initial requirements into a maturely designed reality. If the project requirements have changed, then security risks to the system should continue to be assessed looking for unexpected weaknesses and threats. Security controls are to be selected and documented as to where, when, and how they will be applied to the architectural design of the system. It is at this point when security has formally been applied to the system, that complete consideration has been given to how it affects other business and IT interdependencies$_{12}$. This is the very definition of implementing security early, not waiting until completion, but during development. Software and hardware acceptance testing should then be conducted to validate that the new system matches both functional and security requirements. Complete documentation should accompany all activities in this phase as well as all the other phases.

C. Implementation/Assessment

Utmost care must be practiced once the delivery, installation, or deployment of the new system is established in a critical production environment. The system must undergo a complete certification process and the results sent to the system owner, developer, and other stakeholders. Management will then provide accreditation, marking the final risk decision on the new system as well as how it interacts with other systems in operation$_{13}$.

D. Operations and Maintenance

Once in a production environment, the system now requires strict change and configuration management. Any further monitoring will measure performance, return on investment, and availability$_{14}$.

Core CISSP Concept

Security is to be implemented at every stage of the SDLC, including the last stage: disposal. A disposal team that properly sanitizes media, discards hardware and software, archives critical information, and closes the system reduces the risk of discovering residual data$_{15}$.

Data security officer Nahid has been emailed four documents. The first document contains specifications about a new cutting-edge jet propulsion system developed for sub-orbital flights. The second document contains pre-flight health information about two test pilots. The third document details potential profit earnings from the new propulsion system. The fourth document shows the number of people who are involved in the project.

What would be the most effective way to protect this information?

A. Data Classification
B. Access Control
C. Cryptography
D. Network Security

Exam Strategy and Mentality

The protection controls surrounding information are reflective of its salience for providing value. Not all information is the same, some require more or less security than others[1]. The importance of data can also change over time. Which choice will be able to protect information given its current sensitivity, usage, and criticality levels? Protecting information is not just about confidentiality, it also means the data is unchanged and available throughout its life cycle all the way until the disposal stage[2]. Which choice would have a plan to dispose of data when it has reached its usefulness?

Think Like A Manager

A manager would look for the choice that would protect the company from all vectors, both external and internal. Which choice has the ability to be rolled out for all data types?

Choice A, data classification, could effectively adjust for all these types of documents. The new propulsion system could give the company a competitive edge - this kind of information must be kept confidential. Disclosure of pilot health data may not damage the entire company, but still is something that should be kept private. Information about profit forecasts or workforce totals are not vital to the organization, but sensitive nonetheless.

What could be more effective to protect information than to use identification, authentication, authorization, and accountability methods of access control? Or to have an operating system that practices mandatory, discretionary, or role-based access control, reducing both purposeful or unintentional incidents of disclosure? To use these access control methods, the security profes-

sional would first need to know the importance of the information that is being protected.

Hint: The correct choice is part of an overall life cycle that includes an acquisition, usage, archival, and disposal stage[3].

Cryptographic controls could secure data at rest and in motion with a near-absolute degree of confidentiality. Wouldn't crypto controls be the most effective way to protect the documents from untrusted eyes? If so, how would we know when and why to use which cryptographic cipher? What would determine whether we use DES with Cipher Block Chaining mode or a stronger algorithm such as AES256?

Network security strategies such as firewalls, VLANs, or a dedicated MPLS circuit are strong technical constructs to protect information, though for a price. What would determine the allocation of money, time, and resources spent to implement these technical controls on the four documents? No matter the choice, the information needs to first be organized in some way in order to be effectively protected.

A. Data Classification (Domain 2)

Data classification allows the identification and prioritization of information[4]. In order to know the type of protections, the amount to spend on those protections, and the true value of the information, classification is required. Here are four corporate data classification labels[5] which are required knowledge for the CISSP exam:

Confidential - Could destroy the company or come close to it if disclosed. A "new cutting-edge" propulsion technology could be considered a trade secret as it gives Nahid's company a competitive advantage. Protective controls far beyond the ones for the other documents should be implemented for this type of information.

Private - Can affect an organization adversely if divulged. Health information may not destroy the company if disclosed, but is private user information and should be classified as such.

Sensitive - Sensitive information such as profit earnings and employee headcount are generally not damaging if seen by the public, but requires some protective measures nonetheless.

Public - Disclosure is not preferred, but acquiesced if it occurs.

Core CISSP Concept

Labeled information helps senior management make better decisions. Classification labels are used to determine information sensitivity and what it would cost the company if there is disclosure. Whenever information is created, it should immediately have a meta description[6].

Data classification helps multilevel security systems by permitting only users with the right clearance label and denying anyone else[7].

Think Like A Manager

Managers need to know the classification of data to decide on the strength of a security control, the cost, and the amount of personnel that need to be allocated. A manager must take these variables into account before deciding on the best choice.

B. Access Control (Domain 5)

The concept of access control is to have technical, physical, or administrative controls to make sure information is not seen or changed by unauthorized subjects. As an example, data classification helps to clear the way in deciding whether to have just passwords for users to access certain documents, or to have them go through the additional step of two-factor authentication. As in, more stringent access control methods will be assigned to data with a meta tag of "confidential" than one tagged with "private" or "sensitive"[8].

C. Cryptography (Domain 3)

A multitude of cryptographic controls exist from which to choose, each one with its own price and complexity. Classification labels help to narrow down the decision within budget and resources. For example, classifications help to decide whether to use Perfect Forward Secrecy for an IPSec VPN tunnel, or use the Diffie-Hellman key exchange in Phase 1. It provides the criticality level of data at rest and in motion to determine whether the company should buy Trusted Platform Modules or install software-based encryption.

D. Network Security (Domain 4)

Data classification allows Nahid to decide whether to buy a $100 firewall or one that costs $5,000. It allows insight into whether two junior security engineers will suffice or a senior security engineer has to be hired. The decisions required to secure assets in a network all depend on the value of the data being protected. Nahid also should not have received these documents over email, this in itself could be a breach of confidentiality. A data classification program may have prevented these documents from taking flight from one location to another, instead opting to allow access while stationary.

Core CISSP Concept

Access control methods, encryption algorithms, network security technologies, backup techniques, vulnerability testing, physical security, or software development models are all derivatives of the decisions, policies, and data classifications created by senior management.

In the year 3017, the human empire has made first contact with another intelligent lifeform. A consular ship has been sent to open communications along with some technological, scientific, and historical information exchange through the ship's system. The human ambassadors would like to learn as much information about their alien delegation without giving away too much of their own nature, biology, or defense capabilities. They want to appear friendly, open, and strong without anything to hide. At this point, the humans are unsure whether the aliens are a terrible danger or a unique opportunity. What kind of system access control model should be given to the aliens?

A. Mandatory Access Control (MAC)
B. Discretionary Access Control (DAC)
C. Attribute-Based Access Control (ABAC)
D. Role-Based Access Control (RBAC)

Exam Strategy and Mentality

Because the CISSP exam involves high-level subject matter, the concepts learned in each domain can be applied to a wide span of heterogeneous industries and environments for their information security management. Concepts do not change; they are high-level principles and can address multiple types of enterprise requirements. The context of the question does not matter, only that subjects need access to objects with a few restrictions. It may take a single or hybrid combination of controls for just the right type of access.

Think Like A Manager

The overarching goals, security requirements, culture, customs, and specific mannerisms of a business will determine the type of access control required for subject-to-object coaction.

The humans would like the aliens to feel free to look around the information system, which would serve as a gateway to learning about mankind's entire existence. They want to be careful what they show because this kind of knowledge will reveal human strengths and weaknesses. Decisions must be made, such as would it be better to blatantly restrict and confine the aliens access like in a MAC system? If so, it may insult the aliens or show a lack of trust. How about customizing access rights for each and every file in the database like in DAC? It would certainly allow the beings to only view the files chosen by the human data owners.

Would it help to use conditional attributes like in ABAC? And if using RBAC, it would provide a centrally managed access model with a single set of rights and permissions that can be applied to all those in the group of extraterrestrials.

Information has value. This value determines who can have access to it. Security professionals are not here to help users get access to valuable information; they are here to protect information from unauthorized access. Access control models are most effective when built into the system so it serves as a technical preventative control as part of a layered defense approach.

The most optimal access control model is one that does not expose any information to extraneous entities[1]. The security professional must consider capability, performance, cost, metrics, and the upkeep of an access model[2]. Once implemented, it brings with it the complexities of any new system. The impact of which can affect user productivity throughout the enterprise or be isolated to a single operational function[3]. Use policies, models, and security mechanisms when designing the access control system.

A. Mandatory Access Control

The MAC model is all about keeping secrets, but the humans want to seem open in showing their history without looking too secretive. MAC is the most restrictive form of access control as it significantly scales down the amount of choices a user has when accessing information on an operating system. A user may even know there are many other objects in existence on the system, but they do not have access to anything outside their boundaries. The MAC model is commonly used in government or military environments where confidentiality is of the highest regard. Mandatory access control is a nondiscretionary control as it has a predetermined set of security labels that can only be accessed by those who have the security clearance matching those labels[4]. The humans would not use MAC at all because it is for highly secretive data, which is not the type of information they are trying to present to the aliens in the first place.

B. Discretionary Access Control

Discretionary access allows the flexibility to choose what can be done on an object based on the data owner's discretion. With DAC, subjects given access to information may also be able to pass that information to other subjects. The aliens may have the discretion to provide access to others, change object or system attributes, create a new object, revise current objects, or change the overall guiding rules of the system[5]. The humans do not want the aliens to have this kind of decentralized control as it can lead to unaccounted access and authorization creep. The provisioning of a DAC system would also be time-consuming because of the number of objects (files, folders, and directories) in the system that would have to be assigned an access control list (ACL). These ACLs would need to be dynamically changed in response to any breaches or compromise[6].

Core CISSP Concept

Some driving factors behind access control policies include the principle of need-to-know, least privilege, competency, authority, conflict-of-interest, separation of duties, or investiture[7]. Access mechanisms are used to translate these policies into an access control list.

C. Attribute-Based Access Control

ABAC grants access based on an object's attributes, subject's specific attributes, environmental conditions, and a preconfigured set of policies[8]. With ABAC, the system would need a policy decision and enforcement engine that could grant the aliens access based on these conditions: they hold the role of an official emissary, arrive on unarmed spaceships, and are located at a specific star system at a specific time. Even if it were possible, ABAC is not optimal if subjects and objects are not consistently maintained. Each object would need to have its attributes assigned, updated, modified, and then revoked[9]. The aliens would need their assigned attributes updated if anything changes such as their location, identity, or roles. At this point, not enough dialogue has occurred with the alien contingency to set up an ABAC model. Questions to consider for ABAC[10]:

- Why do we need it? What is the cost? Benefit? Risk? Capabilities?
- How will objects, trust, privileges, and access rules be managed?
- How will business processes change to accommodate ABAC?
- How will interdependencies and interoperability be maintained?
- How will overall ABAC performance be evaluated?

D. Role-Based Access Control

RBAC can make assignment of permissions simple, flexible, and customized[11]. The humans can engineer a role with a narrow set of preselected privileges that can then be assigned or revoked for each member of the alien delegation. Any of the aliens will be free to use their role to navigate and investigate all of mankind's recorded history. However, what the aliens see in their assigned role will differ from the role assigned to humans. The humans can allow the aliens to have a static position of access without the need for dynamic system decisions (policies) like ABAC, a strict environment like MAC, or leave a chance for excess permissions like in DAC. RBAC will reduce administrative overhead by not having to create access for each subject[12]. Consider this: the aliens may also be assigning a role to the humans. They may be hiding their own history, weapons capabilities, or technological advancements. Not as a precaution, but careful as to not overload the capacity of the human brain.

A storage warehouse facility has been taken over by a corporation that will convert it into a data center handling highly classified information in a private cloud. Fences will be built, cameras will be installed, concrete bollards will be erected, and armed security guards will be patrolling the perimeter at all times. Next-generation firewalls, intrusion prevention and detections systems (IPS and IDS), malware scanners, Bell-LaPadula operating systems, and encryption will protect the servers. Policies, procedures, data classification, background checks, credit scores, controlled termination, and a general security awareness program will be applied to all personnel.

What approach to security is being coordinated by the corporation?

A. Defense-in-depth
B. Crime Prevention Through Environmental Design (CPTED)
C. Natural Access Control
D. Target Hardening

Exam Strategy and Mentality

Multiple controls are going to be deployed throughout different locations of the data center facility. The perimeter of the facility will have physical controls, the internal information will have technical controls, and overall administrative controls will be used to align staff members with company hiring requirements. The first set of controls occur outside the warehouse. The second set of controls are applied inside the facility getting closer to the asset, and the third set of controls can be applied throughout the organization. Due care has been performed to cover multiple vectors of compromise.

Hint: Look for the answer that may seem like an assortment of separate controls, but at a high-level are meant to all work in concert with each other.

Defense-in-depth aims to layer defensive controls one after another making it progressively difficult for a variety of attack methods to reach the target[1]. It is meant to deter social engineers from gaining physical access, prevent hackers from making it past the firewall, and account for insider threats who are attempting to access or destroy valued information. Does this sound like what the corporation wants to do for the new data center hosting classified information?

CPTED makes it difficult for an attacker to get away with their actions without being seen by creating an area of high public visibility. Natural surveillance, territorial reinforcement, designated spaces, and scheduled maintenance ensures a place where people practice awareness to prevent crime and maintain security[2]. Is this what the corporation is trying to do? Is CPTED an incomplete approach for the facility?

Natural access control is meant to provide physical security without being too obvious. It is meant to guide people on a general path toward a specific location while discouraging any deviations. An IPS, firewall, encryption cipher, or malware scanners do not achieve this. Fences and bollards could control natural access[3], but they do not protect the actual digital data located in a server, nor can natural access prevent attacks from inside the building. Target hardening is about denying access and not caring whether it is done politely or in a friendly manner[4]. Does this sound like the only type of control being designed for the data center?

Think Like A Manager

Think not that a firewall will protect the asset, but what to do if the firewall fails to do so - if an intruder makes it past the fence, IPS, and the encryption.

A. Defense-in-depth

The concept of defense-in-depth is to have multiple types of controls in place for multiple vectors of compromise. As in, a $50,000 firewall protecting a server is useless if the door to the data center is unlocked. If an armed security guard protecting a laptop is overpowered, hard drive encryption still prevents disclosure of the data. To maximize an organization's security, it is best to use a trifecta of physical, technical, and administrative controls concurrently in a layered approach[5]. Choice A involves all categories of security controls, whereas choices B, C, and D are concerned with just physical security of the outside environment.

Core CISSP Concept

Above all else, the #1 important asset is human life. Protect this asset at all costs. There is no price that can be placed on human safety. BCP/DRP programs, policies, and physical security must all first consider making sure the human heart keeps functioning. Make no exceptions.

In order to protect all human life, critical assets, and remain profitable, a business has to look at themselves from a holistic perspective, from a high-level view. This means to have a strong physical perimeter (fences, biometrics, motion detector, dogs), a network architecture based on a sound security foundation (VPN, web application firewall, WPA2, fiber optics) and a strong set of controls preventing direct access to the asset (access control, encryption, antivirus). The idea being if one control fails to protect the asset, there are multiple other controls that still need to be overcome by an attacker[6].

No amount of defensive controls can ever protect the weakest element in a company to which we also put the most faith: people. To counteract, a manager's best weapons are background checks to look for criminal history, credit score check to view fiscal responsibility, or any other employee screening measures[7]. Security awareness training also provides all users a base level of security understanding on how to react and also how not to react against potential threats[8].

B. Crime Prevention Through Environmental Design

CPTED is about designing a physical environment that directly makes people feel safe and attackers think twice. It is not just for information system facilities but also schools, public bathrooms, parks, or college campuses[9]. A CPTED design will make an attacker strongly consider their choice before committing a crime in an area with a lot of natural surveillance. Examples of CPTED include[10]:

- Adequate lighting around streets or underground structures whereas a person can recognize a face from 10 meters away.
- Stair towers with clear glass walls in parking garages. Individuals may be deterred from criminal acts in visible areas.
- Signs that encourage reporting suspicious or criminal behavior. This informs potential attackers of the neighborhood's vigilance.
- Highly visible ingress/egress points of a neighborhood.

CPTED is not the correct answer because it is a primarily physical security control. Armed security guards are not part of CPTED. The corporation intends to approach the facility with a layered defense that can withstand attackers with multiple types of skills.

C. Natural Access Control

Natural access control is a part of CPTED that uses elements such as lighting, landscaping, or sidewalks to make people feel safe. It is meant to navigate them to where they should be going and away from where they should not be going[11]. Examples include putting in grass lawns to deter vehicles from driving in that area or lighting that illuminates the main pathway to a building entrance.

D. Target Hardening

Target hardening is another component of CPTED that involves the blatant use of physical or man-made boundaries. It is not about making the data center look friendly or welcoming, but a show of force to discourage any trespassers, malicious or otherwise[12]. Although this is being practiced in the question, it still is just a physical control. Choices C and D are components of choice B.

Without prior notification or coordination, Rymar Tech's network engineers changed their firewall's public IP address over the weekend and unexpectedly broke a VPN tunnel to an e-commerce service provider. This meant customers could no longer conduct online shopping purchases, process credit card payments, or access their account. The business managers were made aware of the situation after hearing it directly from escalated customer complaints. They immediately instructed security operations to restore all business processes even if it meant putting functionality over security. Ignoring their directive, the system architects worked with the network team to revert back to the old IP address and restore full connectivity. Moving forward, what kind of changes to the organization can you advise C-level executives to better align IT security with business objectives?

A. Develop an enterprise security architecture
B. Create an Information Security Management System (ISMS)
C. Employ the Zachman Framework
D. Improve strategic alignment

Exam Strategy and Mentality

Communication and procedures do not seem like they are in order at Rymar Tech. Network engineers are doing rogue maintenance work, architects are not listening to their bosses, and managers are making decisions that may impact integrity, confidentiality, availability, or user privacy.

The correct choice will not only fix broken communication channels, but also bring strategic and operational processes together. The solution will make sure that if the exact same problem occurs again, it will be handled more cohesively. Although it may take some time, money, and considerable initial effort, the ultimate solution will actually create a more organized business that can handle sudden changes with ease and a proper governance structure.

Think Like A Manager

There is a glaring element missing at Rymar Tech. Which choice would lay the groundwork for not just IT, but all other departments to understand the business goals?

If the choices all seem unfamiliar, then look at the keywords: "develop", "create", "employ", and "improve". Given the disconnects in the context of the question, does something need to be developed to fix processes, created to align business objectives, employed to connect IT with other departments, or improved on an existing platform? Does an existing solution need to be restructured or is a new initiative required?

Hint: Which choice will be able to align, enable, enhance, and increase security effectiveness?

All the choices seem like they would work to help align IT with the business. If this is true, then the "best" answer is the one that will have the biggest and most long-term positive impact. Which one will not be practiced in just a single silo, but every part of the enterprise? Which choice would work to account for each issue in the question?

A security architecture would allow different parts of the enterprise to be linked together with a common security strategy. An ISMS would outline the controls needed to integrate security throughout the organization. While generic, the Zachman Framework model would provide a flat view of the language necessary to communicate with each type of business audience. Improving strategic alignment brings together the notion for each silo that the business processes take first consideration and everything else comes second.

A. Develop an enterprise security architecture

The development of an enterprise security architecture can merge the gap between IT operations and business processes. It can be used to not only provide a holistic view of the entire organization, but also align all of it together. Security professionals involved in a charette of enterprise architecture will think of interdepartmental standardization, cost-effective design, process solutions, and procedures that will be understood across business units in a language specific to their role[1]. As in, instead of just making their firewall change, the network engineers would have first properly communicated the maintenance work to all relevant departments of the business. A security architecture would educate IT and provide insight into how changes to their systems can take down another revenue generating system. This way even if an incident occurred, stakeholders would be prepared to address it. It is not a good look when managers have to receive bad news from customers instead of their own staff. A security architecture solution would lay the groundwork for establishing proper communication channels in both a bottom-up or top-down approach[2].

It was recommended that for an immediate fix, it would be okay to bypass VPN security, which could compromise confidentiality and integrity. It is important to remember that the business comes first and whatever senior management says to do has to be done; however, security architecture can allow business decision makers to understand and make choices based on security concerns[3]. While security operations resolved the issue, a security architecture would also avoid situations where architects ignore executive instructions and put security over functionality at their own discretion.

Core CISSP Concept

A security architecture comes only after a general architecture. A unifying business architecture focused on converging the relationships between information systems, data, and operational elements of an organization comes before adding on security policies, procedures, and solutions[4].

If one part of the company does not understand how another part works, it is a risk. Suppose management wants to add an expedited shipping process for online purchases, but may not fully understand that their operations department does not have the resources to support such a service. Security architecture reduces disconnect and works to lay out the capabilities and components of each layer of the company beforehand along with the security objectives. When IT has to perform changes or maintenance on their side, it should be in concert with making sure it does not affect the security of other business processes. When the business makes strategic decisions, it should attempt to align with operational and security capability.

B. Create an Information Security Management System

An ISMS describes controls for the management of data, risk, accountability, or physical security. When a security architecture exists, it can take the information from the ISMS and apply it to each business, operations, administrative, and user level[5]. Architecture helps to disperse ISMS controls through each organizational group.

C. Employ the Zachman Framework

The Zachman Framework is one of many enterprise architectures that can be used to communicate the same issue in a language different silos of the business can understand[6]. The framework will answer the same what, how, where, who, when, and why in a language that relates to different departmental perspectives. When a website stops working, executives are concerned with liabilities, assets, clients, partners, milestones, and business strategy. Engineers are about system status, network interfaces, technical designs, and outputs. Same issue, different language. Choice C is a specific framework that enhances an overall architecture, not just security.

D. Improve strategic alignment

IT is here to support the business; the business isn't here for IT. Changing an IP address should not affect what makes the company money. It is more important that customers are making purchases than IT making changes. While a good answer, this choice is too specific and first requires the development of security architecture[7].

A record label's newly created synthesizer software has been deployed to the sound engineers in the music department. The lead producer has asked whether the software can be upgraded to import .WAV files in a compressed format. The developers stated it would be simple and quick to do. They will deploy an upgrade with the ability to compress .WAV files in the next software release schedule, pending approval. Twenty hours after the new software upgrade, the synth program started locking up the media server whenever attempting to import .WAV files. The server became accessible only after the security administrator performed an emergency system restart.

Which due care measure should have been performed first?

A. Change management
B. Regression testing
C. Threat modeling
D. Extreme Programming (XP)

Exam Strategy and Mentality

It may first help to see which choice is about performing due care. Due care means to direct prompt focus on the best thing to do for a certain situation at that given moment. Which choice would have helped the most to perform just before the new software was deployed? Which choice may have detected the reason behind the server locking up?

Was it the absence of change management that failed the company's process? Given the deployment and release schedule already in place, development projects seem to have some measure of existing management and repeatable control - similar to Level 2 of the Capability Maturity Model Integration[1]. Remember that change management and regression testing occur after initial software deployment, while threat modeling and XP occurs beforehand.

Core CISSP Concept

Knowing CISSP processes helps to recognize when one is broken. Look for the choice that would most appropriately fill the gap in the present process. Regression testing exists to make sure any changes to software does not accidentally break system functionality, performance, or protection[2]. Although the server did cease to function and a reboot was urgently required to bring it back online, would such a simple change really warrant conducting a complete regression testing process? Or would it be better to treat it on a per-issue basis and just reboot the server whenever it locks up? Would regression testing provide an acceptable level of confidence for the business need, cost, value, and return on investment of the new software?

Threat modeling can take two forms: one done during risk management and one during software development. Both work to look for the number of probable threats in correlation with existing vulnerabilities, instead of the ones which are just possible[3]. Is this choice a due care measure and could it have detected the software malfunction before it locked up the server?

Extreme Programming is about churning out software at a fast pace while focusing on customer satisfaction as the end result[4]. Constant changes and new requests to the initial software requirements are welcomed and testing is continuously being performed. Should this model have been used for the update to the new compression code?

Hint: Are the choices in chronological order? Does one choice come first then the other when it comes to making a software change?

A. Change management

More changes are occurring within the enterprise now than any other time in telecommunications[5]. Software updates, hotfixes, vulnerability patches, upgrading old devices, failover testing, and firewall rules all require a change management process. It is important to make sure rapid technology changes do not wind up creating unexpected issues once implemented. There must be a formal method to request, design, approve, test, deploy, rollback, and document all changes. Integrity is the primary goal of change management and it is achieved by having multiple eyes verifying that information remains consistent before, during, and after a new change[6]. This is not the correct answer because deploying compression software that is "pending approval" insinuates the developers have an existing change management process in place already. There is a software release schedule to be followed, minimizing ad hoc changes. Change management is a form of due diligence as it is a long-term objective.

B. Regression testing

Regression testing is making sure new code does not alter software that is already in place. Changes to software, however big or small, must be tested before being put into a live enterprise. The idea is not only that regression tests should be performed before making a change that may or may not affect a system, but to just test the overall system once again since initial deployment[7]. A single interactive acceptance test by humans may not always root out flaws hidden deep within the lines of software code[8]. Think of regression testing as not only to check the validation of new code, but also a way to make sure previously corrected development issues are not recurring. This is the correct choice because testing something before deploying it is just a prudent thing to do, which is the definition of due care. For software engineers, regression testing is to make sure the software update is working properly. For managers, it's a way to prevent a disruption to the performance of the business, which could lead to increased cost and lowered productivity. For security professionals, it is to make sure a new change does not inadvertently open up new vulnerabilities or widen existing ones.

The other two types of testing are unit and integration. In unit testing a single part of the overall software is tested, while integration testing determines whether all the parts are able to work together per the design. A combination of both these tests will provide an optimal degree of confidence in the application's ability to reduce risk[9]. Please note: software should never be tested in a production environment.

Think Like A Manager

Code developers should not also be code testers. Separation of duties should be practiced to avoid conflicts of interest where a developer may be hesitant to admit a coding error because of hubris, deadlines, or effort. Different teams should handle the development, testing, and production assimilation of code[10].

C. Threat modeling

The importance of this model is to take into consideration the reasonable types of insider or outsider threats to the application whether in a malicious capacity or in the form of a mistake. Then proceed to map how these probable attacks can be realized with the existing or new vulnerabilities in the software. Threat modeling is a type of due diligence because of the amount of research put in beforehand and is most effective during the design phase of software development[11]. Regression testing is the more accurate answer.

D. Extreme Programming

There is a cute reason for the name of this programming model, it consists of an extreme amount of teamwork. The engineers, senior developers, team leads, managers, and the customers are considered equals in a bid to turn out software as quick as possible[12]. Part of the Agile methodology, XP brings people together without overburdening its developers with a lot of processes to follow[13]. Unit testing may be used in XP at a minimal level as only the minimal amount of code will be used to pass the test. This process could have tested for server lock-ups before deployment. XP provides software releases as fast as possible without a set schedule, making this an incorrect choice. XP is also a software development model that is not a form of due care.

Some of us just want to better ourselves to keep up with our profession, to become a better security professional. Some of us don't get to go home after work and watch an entire series on Netflix or scroll through Instagram. Instead we opt for *Sybex CISSP 8th Edition, CCNA 200-301, Blue Team Field Manual, The TCP/IP Guide, Python Crash Course, AWS Solutions Architect Official Guide*, firewall administration guides, or *Alan Turing: The Enigma*. Some of us go home and read the books that relate to our job function, to try and become an expert at our jobs so we earn the respect of our peers and make our kids proud.

If you want job security, the CISSP is worth it. If you want to spend more time with your family, the CISSP is worth it. If you lose your job and need to get another job fast before your mortgage is due, then the CISSP is worth it. If you are 100% qualified for a high-paying job, but one of the requirements is that you have a CISSP, you don't have to worry about a missed opportunity because you *didn't* have something. If you want to be part of a global community of security professionals (okay maybe you don't need the CISSP for that, but it helps!) the CISSP is worth it. There was so much I didn't know about security before studying for the CISSP. While studying I learned about polyinstantiation, referential integrity, known-plaintext attacks, procedures, policies, ISO 27001, bollards, and one-time pads. I learned the power of mathematics while studying about Diffie-Hellman, the importance of encryption throughout history, the meaning of data remanence, or the different types of fires and how to best extinguish them. Studying for the CISSP, even if you don't pass, helps you correlate the many facets of security and how they all eventually relate to each other. If you want to stop yourself from constantly needing motivation, but instead cultivate a sense of discipline that will follow you for the rest of your life, the CISSP is worth it.

Final Words From Luke

The journey to the CISSP, it's an epic adventure. The harder you study, the more you lessen the fear of failing. In the testing center, when the timer begins to count down, there is nothing to focus on except the computer terminal in front of you presenting deep-level security questions. You take everything you learned in all those thousands of pages of your study guides, all those hours of watching videos, all those days of going over nothing but practice questions, and focus it all into the glow of the monitor. The exam is so intense it is as if you took a breath, and when you exhaled the exam was over; your fate is either a pass or a fail. You have to push yourself to pass this thing, you have to want it more than anything at this point of time in your life.

Imagine the exam ends and you walk toward the testing center proctor, the longest walk you'll ever take, and wait to hear the laboring engine of the printer writing up the destiny of your information security career. You're either going to feel a crushing feeling of disappointment or a warm moment of the impossible realization that you have passed. Whatever the outcome, you're still not the same person that you were just a few hours, days, or months ago. You've improved. You have gained a greater perception of information security concepts than ever before. You can navigate your way around conversations with both technical engineers and C-level executives. You see the reality that nothing is perfect and you can't eliminate every risk. Ultimately, it doesn't really matter if you pass or fail, the journey to the CISSP is the real prize.

By now I've spent over 2,000 nights grinding as a CISSP instructor. Similar to your journey to the CISSP, mine has also been filled with sleepless nights creating CISSP videos, practice questions, flashcards, and managing multiple social media platforms. This whole security thing is not a job, it's a commitment.

I am truly grateful for all those who have allowed me to be a part of their CISSP journey. Your stories inspire me every day.

Thank you all.

-Luke Ahmed

STUDY NOTES AND THEORY

A CISSP Study Guide
www.studynotesandtheory.com

The Study Notes and Theory Members Portal provides custom CISSP videos, practice questions, flashcards, comprehensive PDF notes, and admission to a private Telegram study group.

@Notes_Theory

CISSP Exam Preparation - Study Notes and Theory

"securityengineer"

References

Question 1

1 "CISSP Computerized Adaptive Testing." CISSP Computerized Adaptive Testing, (ISC)², www.isc2.org/Certifications/CISSP/CISSP-CAT.

2, 3, 4, 5, 10 Kissel, Richard, et al. "Guidelines for Media Sanitization NIST Special Publication 800-88." Guidelines for Media Sanitization, National Institute of Standards and Technology, Sept. 2006, tsapps.nist.gov/publication/get_pdf.cfm?pub_id=50819.

6 Gordon, Adam. Official (ISC)² Guide to the CISSP CBK ((ISC)² Press). 4th ed. Taylor and Francis Group, LLC. 2015.

7, 8 Chapple, Mike, and James M Stewart. (ISC)² CISSP Certified Information Systems Security Professional Official Study Guide. 8th ed., Wiley, 2018.

9 Harris, Shon. and Maymi, Fernando. CISSP All-in-One Exam Guide, 7th Edition. 7th ed. New York: McGraw-Hill, 2016.

Question 2

1 "Primary: Definition of Primary by Lexico." Lexico Dictionaries | English, Lexico Dictionaries. Powered by Oxford., 2020, www.lexico.com/en/definition/primary.

2, 3 Chapple, Mike, and James M Stewart. (ISC)² CISSP Certified Information Systems Security Professional Official Study Guide. 8th ed., Wiley, 2018.

4 "ICGN Guidance on Corporate Risk Oversight." ICGN International Corporate Governance Network, ICGN International Corporate Governance Network, 2015, www.icgn.org/sites/default/files/ICGN%20Corp%20Risk%20Oversightweb_0.pdf.

5, 6, 7, 8 "Guide for Conducting Risk Assessments - NIST." National Institute of Standards and Technology, National Institute of Standards and Technology, Sept. 2012, nvlpubs.nist.gov/nistpubs/Legacy/SP/nistspecialpublication800-30r1.pdf.

Question 3

1, 5, 6, 7 Harris, Shon. and Maymi, Fernando. CISSP All-in-One Exam Guide, 7th Edition. 7th ed. New York: McGraw-Hill, 2016

2, 4, 8, 9, 10 Chapple, Mike, and James M Stewart. (ISC)² CISSP Certified Information Systems Security Professional Official Study Guide. 8th ed., Wiley, 2018.

3 McCormack, George. "Data Users." Outcome 1: Describe the Legislation That Applies to the IT Profession, Higher National Computing: E-Learning Materials, Mar. 2008, www.sqa.org.uk/e-learning/ITLaw01CD/page_19.htm.

11 Sagan, Carl, 1934-1996. Carl Sagan's Cosmic Connection : an Extraterrestrial Perspective. Cambridge ; New York: Cambridge University Press, 2000.

Question 4

1 Harris, Shon. and Maymi, Fernando. CISSP All-in-One Exam Guide, 7th Edition. 7th ed. New York: McGraw-Hill, 2016.

2, 3, 4, 5, 6 NIST 800-15 Scarfone, Karen, et al. "Technical Guide to Information Security Testing and Assessment." National Institute of Standards and Technology, National Institute of Standards and Technology, Sept. 2008, nvlpubs.nist.gov/nistpubs/Legacy/SP/nistspecialpublication800-115.pdf.

7 Eltringham, Scott. "Prosecuting Computer Crimes." The United States Department of Justice, Office of Legal Education Executive Office for United States Attorneys, 14 Jan. 2015, www.justice.gov/sites/default/files/criminal-ccips/legacy/2015/01/14/ccmanual.pdf.

8 Daniel Regalado. Shon Harris. Allen Harper. Chris Eagle. Jonathan Ness. Branko Spasojevic. Ryan Linn. Stephen Sims. Gray Hat Hacking The Ethical Hacker's Handbook, Fourth Edition. McGraw-Hill/Osborne, 2015.

Question 5

1 Puttygen.com

2, 3, 4, 10 Harris, Shon. and Maymi, Fernando. CISSP All-in-One Exam Guide, 7th Edition. 7th ed. New York: McGraw-Hill, 2016.

5, 6, 8, 9 Chapple, Mike, and James M Stewart. (ISC)² CISSP Certified Information Systems Security Professional Official Study Guide. 8th ed., Wiley, 2018.

7 "Guidelines on Firewalls and Firewall Policy." Computer Security Resource Center, National Institute of Standards and Technology, Sept. 2009, csrc.nist.gov/publications/detail/sp/800-41/rev-1/final.

Question 6

1 "Code of Ethics: Complaint Procedures: Committee Members." Code of Ethics | Complaint Procedures | Committee Members, 2020, www.isc2.org/Ethics.

2, 3, Harris, Shon. and Maymi, Fernando. CISSP All-in-One Exam Guide, 7th Edition. 7th ed. New York: McGraw-Hill, 2016.

4, 8, 10 "Why Is Third Party Risk Management Important?" Third Party Risk Management Managing Risks in Your Extended Enterprise, Deloitte, 2017, www2.deloitte.com/content/dam/Deloitte/sg/Documents/risk/sg-risk-third-party-risk-management-brochure.pdf.

5, 7, 9 Gordon, Adam. Official (ISC)² Guide to the CISSP CBK ((ISC)2 Press). 4th ed. Taylor and Francis Group, LLC. 2015.

11 Chapple, Mike, and James M Stewart. (ISC)² CISSP Certified Information Systems Security Professional Official Study Guide. 8th ed., Wiley, 2018.

6 "CMMI Institute." CMMI Institute - CMMI Levels of Capability and Performance, ISACA, 2020, cmmiinstitute.com/learning/appraisals/levels.

Question 7

1, 3, 4, 6, 7, 8, 9 Harris, Shon. and Maymi, Fernando. CISSP All-in-One Exam Guide, 7th Edition. 7th ed. New York: McGraw-Hill, 2016.

2, 5 Blake, Sonya. "The Clark-Wilson Security Model." Global Information Assurance Certification Paper, Global Information Assurance Certification Paper, 17 May 2000, www.giac.org/paper/gsec/835/clark-wilson-security-model/101747.

Question 8

5, 16, 17 Harris, Shon. and Maymi, Fernando. CISSP All-in-One Exam Guide, 7th Edition. 7th ed. New York: McGraw-Hill, 2016.

3, 4, 6, 7, 8, 10, 11, 12, 14 Chapple, Mike, and James M Stewart. (ISC)² CISSP Certified Information Systems Security Professional Official Study Guide. 8th ed., Wiley, 2018.

1, 2, 15 "DDoS Quick Guide." National Cybersecurity and Communications Integration Center, National Cybersecurity and Communications Integration Center, 29 Jan. 2014, www.us-cert.gov/sites/default/files/publications/DDoS%20Quick%20Guide.pdf.

9 Specht, Stephen, and Ruby Lee. "Taxonomies of Distributed Denial of Service Networks, Attacks, Tools, and Countermeasures." Taxonomies of Distributed Denial of Service Networks, Attacks, Tools, and Countermeasures, Princeton Architecture Laboratory for Multimedia and Security, 16 May 2003, www.princeton.edu/~rblee/ELE572Papers/Fall04Readings/DDoSSurveyPaper_20030516_Final.pdf.

13 Real-world experience

Question 9

1 Harris, Shon. and Maymi, Fernando. CISSP All-in-One Exam Guide, 7th Edition. 7th ed. New York: McGraw-Hill, 2016.

2 "Art. 50 GDPR - International Cooperation for the Protection of Personal Data." GDPR.eu, General Data Protection Regulation (GDPR), 14 Nov. 2018, gdpr.eu/article-50-countries-outside-of-europe-cooperation/.

3 "Art. 17 GDPR - Right to Erasure ('Right to Be Forgotten')." GDPR.eu, General Data Protection Regulation (GDPR), 14 Nov. 2018, gdpr.eu/article-17-right-to-be-forgotten/.

4 "Art. 34 GDPR - Communication of a Personal Data Breach to the Data Subject." GDPR.eu, General Data Protection Regulation, 14 Nov. 2018, gdpr.eu/article-34-communication-of-a-personal-data-breach/.

5, 9 "Tokenization Product Security Guidelines – Irreversible and Reversible Tokens." Tokenization Product Security Guidelines, PCI Security Standards Council, Apr. 2015, www.pcisecuritystandards.org/documents/Tokenization_Product_Security_Guidelines.pdf.

6, "All You Need to Know about Tokenization." All You Need to Know about Tokenization, VISA Inc., usa.visa.com/dam/VCOM/download/security/documents/visa-security-tokenization-infographic.pdf.

7, 10 Chapple, Mike, and James M Stewart. (ISC)² CISSP Certified Information Systems Security Professional Official Study Guide. 8th ed., Wiley, 2018.

8, 12 Harris, Shon. and Maymi, Fernando. CISSP All-in-One Exam Guide, 7th Edition. 7th ed. New York: McGraw-Hill, 2016.

11 McCallister, Erika, et al. "Guide to Protecting the Confidentiality of Personally Identifiable Information (PII)." Recommendations of the National Institute of Standards and Technology, National Institute of Standards and Technology, Apr. 2010, nvlpubs.nist.gov/nistpubs/Legacy/SP/nistspecialpublication800-122.pdf.

Question 10

1 Mell, Peter, and Timothy Grance. "The NIST Definition of Cloud Computing." Recommendations of the National Institute of Standards and Technology, National Institute of Standards and Technology, Sept. 2011, nvlpubs.nist.gov/nistpubs/Legacy/SP/nistspecialpublication800-145.pdf.

2, 3, 4, 5 Jansen, Wayne, and Timothy Grance. "Guidelines on Security and Privacy in Public Cloud Computing." Guidelines on Security and Privacy in Public Cloud Computing, National Institute of Standards and Technology, Dec. 2011, nvlpubs.nist.gov/nistpubs/Legacy/SP/nistspecialpublication800-144.pdf.

Question 11

1, 2, Harris, Shon. and Maymi, Fernando. CISSP All-in-One Exam Guide, 7th Edition. 7th ed. New York: McGraw-Hill, 2016.

3 Gordon, Adam. Official (ISC)² Guide to the CISSP CBK ((ISC)² Press). 4th ed. Taylor and Francis Group, LLC. 2015.

4, 6, 7, 8 Chapple, Mike, and James M Stewart. (ISC)² CISSP Certified Information Systems Security Professional Official Study Guide. 8th ed., Wiley, 2018.

5 Swanson, Marianne, et al. "NIST Special Publication (SP) 800-18 Rev. 1, Guide for ..." Guide for Developing Security Plans for

Federal Information Systems, National Institute of Standards and Technology, Feb. 2006, csrc.nist.gov/publications/detail/sp/800 -18/rev-1/final.

Question 12

1 Hoffman, P., and B. Schneier. "Doc: RFC 4270: Attacks on Cryptographic Hashes in Internet Protocols." Attacks on Cryptographic Hashes in Internet Protocols, Network Working Group, Nov. 2005, www.hjp.at/doc/rfc/rfc4270.html.

2, 3, 4, 5, 6, 8, 9, 10, 11 Harris, Shon. and Maymi, Fernando. CISSP All-in-One Exam Guide, 7th Edition. 7th ed. New York: McGraw-Hill, 2016.

7 Chapple, Mike, and James M Stewart. (ISC)² CISSP Certified Information Systems Security Professional Official Study Guide. 8th ed., Wiley, 2018.

Question 13

1, 8 Chapple, Mike, and James M Stewart. (ISC)² CISSP Certified Information Systems Security Professional Official Study Guide. 8th ed., Wiley, 2018.

2, 3, 4, 6, 7 Harris, Shon. and Maymi, Fernando. CISSP All-in-One Exam Guide, 7th Edition. 7th ed. New York: McGraw-Hill, 2016.

5 Swanson, Marianne, et al. "Contingency Planning Guide for Federal Information Systems ." National Institute of Standards and Technology Special Publication 800-34, National Institute of Standards and Technology, May 2010, nvlpubs.nist.gov/nistpubs /Legacy/SP/nistspecialpublication800-34r1.pdf.

Question 14

1, 2, 4, 5, 6 Chapple, Mike, and James M Stewart. (ISC)² CISSP Certified Information Systems Security Professional Official Study Guide. 8th ed., Wiley, 2018.

3 "Firewall Interfaces Overview." Firewall Interfaces Overview, Palo Alto Networks, 30 Apr. 2020, docs.paloaltonetworks.com/ pan-os/8-1/pan-os-web-interface-help/network/network-interfaces/firewall-interfaces-overview.

Question 15

1 "NIST Risk Management Framework Overview." NIST Risk Management Framework Overview, National Institute of Standards and Technology, 28 Mar. 2018, www.nist.gov/system/ files/documents/2018/03/28/vickie_nist_risk_management_ framework_overview-hpc.pdf.

2 Xu, William; Grant, Gerald; Nguyen, Hai; and Dai, Xianyi (2008) "Security Breach: The Case of TJX Companies, Inc.," Communica-

tions of the Association for Information Systems: Vol. 23, Article 31.

3 Chapple, Mike, and James M Stewart. (ISC)² CISSP Certified Information Systems Security Professional Official Study Guide. 8th ed., Wiley, 2018.

4, 5, 6 Gordon, Adam. Official (ISC)² Guide to the CISSP CBK ((ISC)² Press). 4th ed. Taylor and Francis Group, LLC. 2015.

Question 16

7 Gordon, Adam. Official (ISC)² Guide to the CISSP CBK ((ISC)² Press). 4th ed. Taylor and Francis Group, LLC. 2015.

1, 2, 3, 4, 5, 6, Harris, Shon. and Maymi, Fernando. CISSP All-in-One Exam Guide, 7th Edition. 7th ed. New York: McGraw-Hill, 2016.

8 Chapple, Mike, and James M Stewart. (ISC)2 CISSP Certified Information Systems Security Professional Official Study Guide. 8th ed., Wiley, 2018.

Question 17

1 2 3 5 6 9 10 Harris, Shon. and Maymi, Fernando. CISSP All-in-One Exam Guide, 7th Edition. 7th ed. New York: McGraw-Hill, 2016.

4 Chapple, Mike, and James M Stewart. (ISC)² CISSP Certified Information Systems Security Professional Official Study Guide. 8th ed., Wiley, 2018.

7 8 Gordon, Adam. Official (ISC)² Guide to the CISSP CBK ((ISC)² Press). 4th ed. Taylor and Francis Group, LLC. 2015.

Question 18

1, 2 Chew, Elizabeth, et al. "I N F O R M A T I O N   S E C U R I T Y." Performance Measurement Guide for Information Security, National Institute of Standards and Technology, July 2008, nvlpubs.nist.gov/nistpubs/Legacy/SP/nistspecialpublication800 -55r1.pdf.

3 Chapple, Mike, and James M Stewart. (ISC)² CISSP Certified Information Systems Security Professional Official Study Guide. 8th ed., Wiley, 2018.

Question 19

1 2 7 8 Scarfone, Karen, et al. "Technical Guide to Information Security Testing and Assessment." Special Publication 800-115, National Institute of Standards and Technology, Sept. 2008, nvlpubs.nist.gov/nistpubs/Legacy/SP/nistspecialpublication800 -115.pdf.

3 9 Chapple, Mike, and James M Stewart. (ISC)² CISSP Certified Information Systems Security Professional Official Study Guide. 8th ed., Wiley, 2018.

4 5 6 11 12 13 Harris, Shon. and Maymi, Fernando. CISSP All-in-One Exam Guide, 7th Edition. 7th ed. New York: McGraw-Hill, 2016.

10 "Combating the Insider Threat." National Cybersecurity and Communications Integration Center, US Department of Homeland Security, 2 May 2014, www.us-cert.gov/sites/default/files/publications/Combating%20the%20Insider%20Threat_0.pdf.

Question 20

1 2 3 4 5 7 8 10 11 12 14 15Kissel, Richard, et al. "Security Considerations in the System Development Life Cycle." NIST Special Publication 800-64 Revision 2, National Institute of Standards and Technology, Oct. 2008, nvlpubs.nist.gov/nistpubs/Legacy/SP/nistspecialpublication800-64r2.pdf.

9 13 Harris, Shon. and Maymi, Fernando. CISSP All-in-One Exam Guide, 7th Edition. 7th ed. New York: McGraw-Hill, 2016.

6 https://cve.mitre.org/cve/

Question 21

1 2 3 4 5 6 8 Harris, Shon. and Maymi, Fernando. CISSP All-in-One Exam Guide, 7th Edition. 7th ed. New York: McGraw-Hill, 2016.

7 "Security and Privacy Controls for Federal Information Systems and Organizations." NIST Special Publication 800-53, National Institute of Standards and Technology, Apr. 2013, nvlpubs.nist.gov/nistpubs/SpecialPublications/NIST.SP.800-53r4.pdf.

Question 22

1 2 3 7 Hu, Vincent, et al. "Assessment of Access Control Systems." Assessment of Access Control Systems, National Institute of Standards and Technology, Sept. 2006, nvlpubs.nist.gov/nistpubs/Legacy/IR/nistir7316.pdf.

4 11 12 Harris, Shon. and Maymi, Fernando. CISSP All-in-One Exam Guide, 7th Edition. 7th ed. New York: McGraw-Hill, 2016.

5 6 "Security and Privacy Controls for Federal Information Systems and Organizations." NIST Special Publication 800-53, National Institute of Standards and Technology, Apr. 2013, nvlpubs.nist.gov/nistpubs/SpecialPublications/NIST.SP.800-53r4.pdf.

8 9 10 Hu, Vincent C, et al. "Guide to Attribute Based Access Control (ABAC) Definition and Considerations." NIST Special Publication 800-162, National Institute of Standards and Technology, Jan. 2014, nvlpubs.nist.gov/nistpubs/specialpublications/NIST.SP.800-162.pdf.

Question 23

1 5 8 Chapple, Mike, and James M Stewart. (ISC)2 CISSP Certified Information Systems Security Professional Official Study Guide. 8th ed., Wiley, 2018.

2 10 11 12 Hoon, Tan. "CRIME PREVENTION THROUGH ENVIRONMENTAL DESIGN." National Crime Prevention Council, National Crime Prevention Council, Oct. 2003, rems.ed.gov/docs/Mobile_docs/CPTED-Guidebook.pdf.

3 4 9 Harris, Shon. and Maymi, Fernando. CISSP All-in-One Exam Guide, 7th Edition. 7th ed. New York: McGraw-Hill, 2016.

6 Barnum, Sean, et al. "Defense in Depth." Cybersecurity and Infrastructure Security Agency CISA, United States Computer Emergency Readiness Team, 2005, www.us-cert.gov/bsi/articles/knowledge/principles/defense-in-depth.

7 McGuiness, Todd. "Defense In Depth." Information Security Reading Room, SANS Institute, 7 May 2020, www.sans.org/reading-room/whitepapers/basics/defense-in-depth-525.

Question 24

1 2 3 4 5 6 7 Harris, Shon. and Maymi, Fernando. CISSP All-in-One Exam Guide, 7th Edition. 7th ed. New York: McGraw-Hill, 2016.

Question 25

1 https://cmmiinstitute.com/learning/appraisals/levels

2 3 9 10 13 Harris, Shon. and Maymi, Fernando. CISSP All-in-One Exam Guide, 7th Edition. 7th ed. New York: McGraw-Hill, 2016.

4 12 extremeprogramming.org

5 6 11 Gordon, Adam. Official (ISC)² Guide to the CISSP CBK ((ISC)² Press). 4th ed. Taylor and Francis Group, LLC. 2015.

7 8 Libes, Don. "Regression Testing and Conformance Testing Interactive Programs." Testing Interactive Programs, National Institute of Standards and Technology, 12 June 1992, tsapps.nist.gov/publication/get_pdf.cfm?pub_id=821305.

About the Author

Luke Ahmed is a CISSP instructor and the founder of Study Notes and Theory. He provides a different way to study for the CISSP exam by striving to come up with a casual and conducive learning environment using a mix of high-level concepts and technical terminology. Luke is a perpetual optimist dedicated to helping those on their journey to the CISSP and becoming a better security professional.

Made in the USA
Middletown, DE
13 February 2022